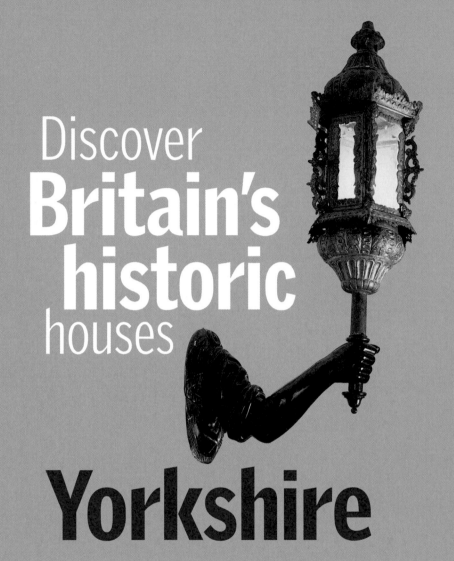

Discover
**Britain's
historic**
houses

Yorkshire

Discover Britain's

Published by Reader's Digest Association Ltd
London • New York • Sydney • Montreal

Reader's Digest

historic houses
Yorkshire

Simon Jenkins

Contents

North York Moors
National Park

Turner's Hospital
atham
SBROUGH
nesby
A174
A171
Runswick Bay
esby Hall
A171
Whitby
9 Banqueting Hall
Lealholm
Robin Hood's Bay
Beck Hole
Ravenscar
A171
A169
Scarborough
Hutton-le-Hole
Ryedale 16 Folk Museum
A64
Lockton
RKSHIRE
ey 15
abx
Helmsley
A170
Thornton-le-Dale
Pickering
A170
Filey
19 Helmsley Castle
18 Park
Nunnington
25 Nunnington Hall
A169
Staxton
A1039
Shandy Hall
Swinton 26 Park
Scampston Hall
27 Scampston
A64
A165
Hovingham 24 Hovingham Hall
Swinton
Old Malton
Malton
Thwing
Sewerby Hall 4
Flamborough
Sewerby
dsby
34 Castle Howard
Bridlington
Burton Agnes Hall
Burton Agnes 2 Manor House 3
on- rest
42 ark
Sledmere
Burton Agnes
Sledmere House 1
brough gh
A1237
Harton
Brockfield Hall
A166
Fridaythorpe
Little Driffield
Driffield
Lissett
43 Warthill
YORK
Kexby
Bar Convent Museum
Barley Hall
Clifford Tower
A614
Bainton
A65
Watton
EAST RIDING
ugh
YORK CITY
Deighton
Fairfax House
Jorvik Viking Centre
The Kings' Manor
Mansion House
Merchant Adventurers' Hall
Middlethorpe Hall
St William's College
Treasurer's House
York Castle Museum
A1079
Hornsea
A1079
A1035
A165
Beverley
West Newton
Skirlaugh
5 Burton Constable Hall
Selby
A19
A1041
Moor End
A1034
Cottingham
North Cave
South Cave
A164
Roos
Maister House
6 Wilberforce House
7
Withernsea
Balkholme
KINGSTON UPON HULL
Hedon
A63
A1033
Keyingham
Patrington
Carlton
Carlton Towers
A645
46
Goole
Easington
Kilnsea
Askern
Thorne
M180
Mansion House
4 DONCASTER
RE
M18

The best in Britain

SCOTLAND

- 125 Blair Castle
- 129 Cawdor Castle
- 126 Craigievar Castle
- 112 Drumlanrig Castle
- 122 Duart Castle
- 130 Dunrobin Castle
- 128 Dunvegan Castle
- 116 Edinburgh Castle
- 127 Eilean Donan Castle
- 115 Floors Castle
- 124 Glamis Castle
- 118 Hopetoun House
- 121 Inveraray Castle
- 117 Linlithgow Palace
- 114 Mellerstain
- 119 Palace of Holyroodhouse
- 123 Scone Palace
- 131 Skara Brae
- 120 Stirling Castle

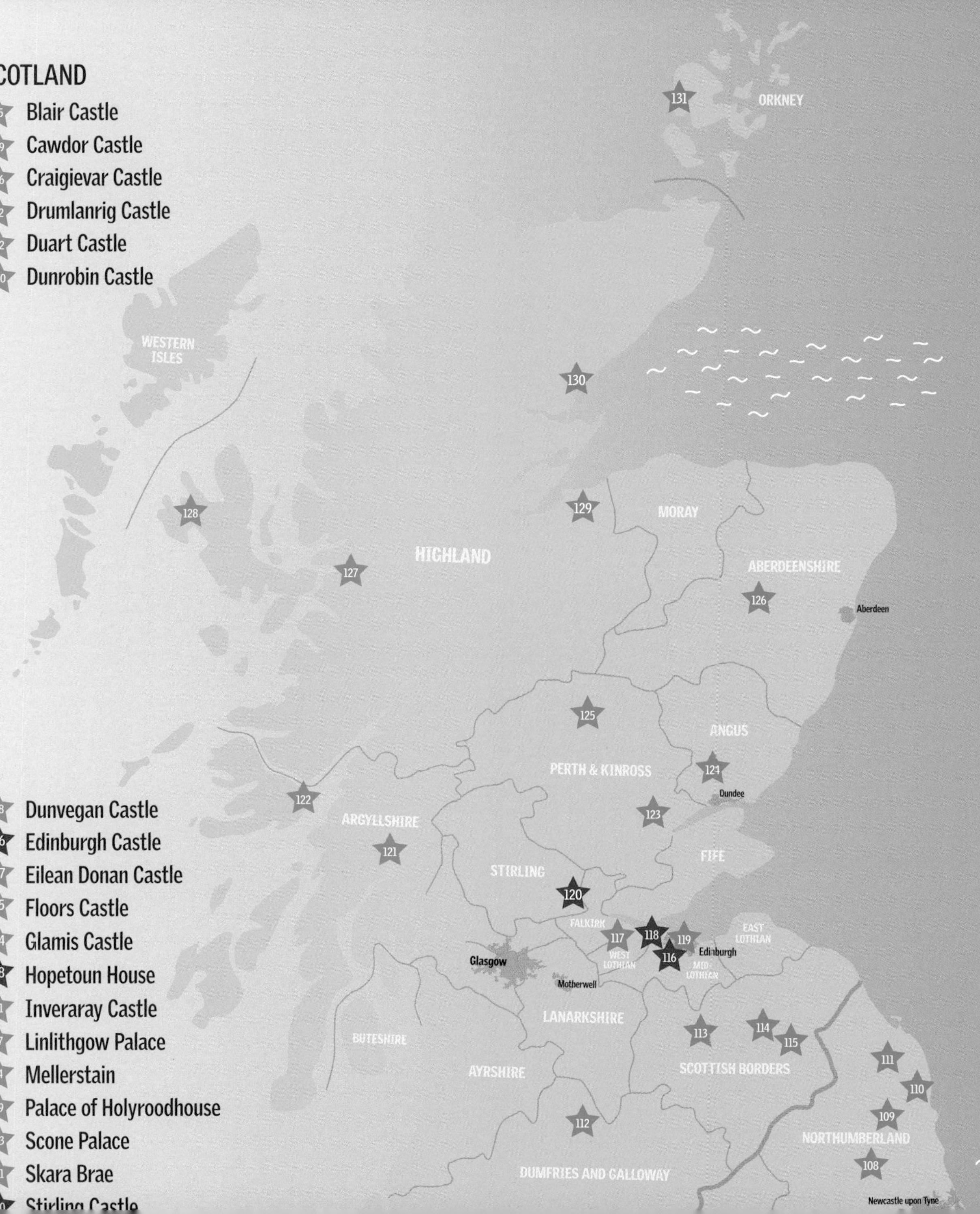

ORKNEY
WESTERN ISLES
HIGHLAND
MORAY
ABERDEENSHIRE
Aberdeen
ANGUS
PERTH & KINROSS
Dundee
ARGYLLSHIRE
FIFE
STIRLING
FALKIRK
EAST LOTHIAN
Edinburgh
WEST LOTHIAN
MID-LOTHIAN
Glasgow
Motherwell
LANARKSHIRE
BUTESHIRE
AYRSHIRE
SCOTTISH BORDERS
NORTHUMBERLAND
DUMFRIES AND GALLOWAY
Newcastle upon Tyne
131
130
129
128
127
126
125
124
123
122
121
120
119
118
117
116
115
114
113
112
111
110
109
108

- 102 Castle Howard
- 14 Charleston
- 56 Chastleton
- 91 Chatsworth House
- 111 Chillingham Castle
- 36 Chiswick House
- 48 Claydon House
- 16 Cothay Manor
- 109 Cragside
- 70 Deene Park
- 38 Dennis Severs House
- 28 Dyrham Park
- 53 Eastnor Castle
- 40 Eltham Palace
- 100 Fairfax House
- 13 Firle Place
- 3 Forde Abbey
- 27 Godinton Park
- 8 Goodwood House
- 78 Grimsthorpe Castle
- 90 Haddon Hall
- 64 Hagley Hall
- 35 Ham House
- 34 Hampton Court
- 93 Hardwick Hall
- 98 Harewood House
- 76 Harlaxton Manor
- 63 Harvington Hall
- 51 Hatfield House
- 22 Hever Castle
- 80 Holkham Hall
- 37 Home House
- 79 Houghton Hall
- 107 Hutton-in-the-Forest
- 25 Ightham Mote
- 74 Kedleston Hall
- 21 Kensington Palace
- 5 Kingston Lacy
- 50 Knebworth House
- 24 Knole
- 29 Lacock Abbey
- 1 Lanhydrock
- 26 Leeds Castle
- 104 Levens Hall
- 19 Longleat
- 89 Lyme Park
- 54 Madresfield Court
- 46 Magdalen College
- 17 Montacute House
- 101 Newby Hall
- 94 Newstead Abbey
- 96 Nostell Priory
- 6 Osborne House
- 32 Osterley Park
- 72 Oxburgh Hall
- 10 Parham House
- 23 Penshurst Place
- 9 Petworth House
- 106 Raby Castle
- 55 Ragley Hall

★ 5 Star
★ 4 Star

I visited these buildings after writing a book on English churches and the experience was as moving as it was different. While places of worship were built according to the authority and liturgy of the Church, people built houses for themselves. A house was useful first and beautiful second. From this derives the joy of visiting English houses. They are a conversation between utility and beauty down the ages.

For me this was a voyage of discovery, and in defining the word 'house' I soon found that I could not sensibly distinguish castle from palace, house from hut, roof from ruin. My list embraces any structure in which men and women have laid their heads, provided that they are in some degree accessible to public view. The selection is a personal list and the commentary is a personal vision, warts and all.

Simon Jenkins

Historic houses
of Yorkshire

This book tells the story not just of the grand homes of Yorkshire but of habitations of all sorts. Yorkshire covers a vast area and its varied landscapes, towns and cities hold many treasures to be discovered. The region is divided into four counties and the chapters of this book follow these divisions with an additional chapter on the city of York.

The **East Riding** lies where the flatlands of eastern England peter out north of the Humber. Once briefly Humberside, the county is the Cinderella of the North, but in houses, as in churches, it makes up in quality what it lacks in quantity. East Riding is almost without houses of the medieval or early Tudor periods, apart from a fragment at Burton Agnes Manor. Yet it has two masterpieces from the Elizabethan-Jacobean watershed – Burton Constable Hall and Robert Smythson's Burton Agnes Hall. The latter ranks

among the finest, and best-presented, houses in England. The county's chief city, Hull, retains an enclave of mercantile houses of the 17th and 18th centuries, well represented by Wilberforce House, with its eccentric Jacobean façade, and the remarkable staircase of the Maister House. Sledmere, after its fire, is a fine restoration.

North Yorkshire is one of England's loveliest counties and richly endowed with houses. The uplands of the Dales and the North York Moors long attracted both castles and monasteries. Great keeps survive at Helmsley, Middleham and Richmond. There are rare medieval courtyard castles at Bolton and Skipton, and incomparable relics of monastic domestic architecture at Fountains and Rievaulx. Markenfield is a picturesque fortified manor. The Tudors left less in Yorkshire than in Lancashire, or perhaps their descendants replaced more. The long gallery at Newburgh is derelict and the tower at Ripley a fragment. Only Smythson's Fountains Hall is a remarkable Elizabethan work, and it was not built until the Queen was dead.

Yorkshire comes into its own with English Baroque and Vanbrugh's majestic palace for the Earl of Carlisle at Castle Howard, and the lesser house that it inspired at Duncombe. Both lent themselves to great landscape architecture. The Palladians contributed eccentric Hovingham and Robert Adam produced at Newby Hall one of his best rooms in England. Other gems include the Grand Tour hall at Beningbrough, Nicholas Stone's chimneypiece at Newburgh, and the tortoiseshell tea-room at Sutton. And James Herriot's house in Thirsk is one of the best renderings of a 1950s interior in England.

The city of **York** has England's finest concentration of historic buildings outside Oxford and Cambridge. Medieval hall houses include the Merchant Adventurers' Hall, King's Manor and St William's College. Both Jorvik and Castle Museum have excellent 'living displays'. Fairfax House is pre-eminent among Georgian town houses, and the Treasurer's House is an immaculate late-Victorian revival.

South Yorkshire was carved in the 1970s from parts of the West and East Ridings and has since relapsed into the Sheffield–Doncaster conurbation. It is not England's happiest landscape, yet it boasts one of England's most intact Norman keeps at Conisbrough. Outside Barnsley two early 18th-century palaces can be seen at Wentworth Woodhouse and Wentworth Castle, where Rockinghams and Straffords vied for architectural glory. Both await full accessibility. The Georgian Mansion House at Doncaster is a civic gem, while Victorian sobriety is displayed at 19th-century Brodsworth.

West Yorkshire is a fine rolling landscape, but the concentrated Victorian mill towns, with their tall chimneys and Florentine municipal buildings, have mostly, and sadly, been replaced by tower blocks and estates showing little respect for the contours that defined earlier settlements. The Middle Ages left a few fragments of military and ecclesiastical architecture, notably the Cistercian Kirkstall Abbey. A good pele survives, astonishingly, within Bolling Hall in Bradford and an unexpected medieval house is emerging at Longley in Huddersfield. The Jacobean era is well represented, with fine yeomen's houses at Oakwell, Shibden and East Riddlesden. Towering over the county is the Ingrams' Temple Newsam, restored to its old glory by the City of Leeds. West Yorkshire has less to show for the 18th century, but Harewood and Nostell are splendour enough, with Adam at his most prolific in both houses and Capability Brown at his most spectacular.

✫ STAR RATINGS AND ACCESSIBILITY ✫✫✫✫✫

The 'star' ratings are entirely my personal choice (but see note below). They rate the overall quality of the house as presented to the public, and not gardens or other attractions. On balance I scaled down houses, however famous, for not being easily accessible or for being only partly open.

The top rating, five stars, is given to those houses that qualify as 'international' celebrities. Four stars are awarded to houses of outstanding architectural quality and public display. Three-star houses comprise the run of good historic houses, well displayed and worthy of national promotion. Two and one-star houses are of more local interest, are hard to visit, or have just one significant feature.

Accessibility varies greatly, from buildings that are open all year to houses that can only be visited 'by appointment' (rarely, I have broken my rule and included a private property that is not open at all, but is viewable from nearby walks or public gardens). Opening hours tend to alter from year to year, but an indication of how accessible a house is to visitors is given at the start of each entry, together with brief information on location and ownership. Many of the houses are National Trust or English Heritage properties, some are now museums or hotels, others are privately owned by families who open to the public for part of the year (English Heritage grant requirements insist on 28 days minimum). Some owners may, understandably, seek to cluster visitors on particular days. More details for each house are given at the back of the book, and readers are advised to check before visiting.

A final note, houses are, or should be, living things subject to constant change and how we view them is bound to be a subject of debate. I welcome any correction or comment, especially from house owners, sent to me c/o the publisher.

NOTE: On the UK map (pages 6-7) the 4 and 5 star houses in England were selected by Simon Jenkins. Those in Scotland and Wales were selected by the editors of Reader's Digest.

Architectural timeline
and Yorkshire's houses in brief

Aske Hall
A mainly Georgian house with evidence of earlier buildings and a medieval pele tower. Magnificent Victorian stables, by Thomas Olliver, grace the grounds.

Bar Convent Museum
A Georgian town house in York. Once a girls' school, it is still home to a convent, as well as a museum, conference centre, library and bed-and-breakfast accommodation.

Barden Tower
The house was restored in the 17th century, being re-built around a ruined pele tower. Today, the house is one more a ruin.

Barley Hall
A reconstruction of a medieval hall house, based on archaeological research and built on the site of a former Lord Mayor of York's home, c1400.

Beningbrough Hall
An early Georgian red-brick house inspired by the original owner's Grand Tour of Italy and designed by William Thornton.

Bolton Castle
A medieval castle, parts of which are ruined. Many rooms have been restored, the south-west tower, which remains complete, includes a good example of a solar.

Bradford: Bolling Hall
A mainly Jacobean house with a surviving medieval pele tower and additions by John Carr of York in the 18th century

Bramham Park
A Queen Anne house set in a formal landscaped garden, where temples, statuary and other structures form focal points on intersecting vistas.

Brockfield Hall
A charmingly elegant Regency house with splendid oval hall and staircase. An impressive Venetian window sits above the entrance.

Brodsworth Hall
A grand Victorian mansion, built c1860 in an Italianate style by the architect Philip Wilkinson, with interiors by the Italian, Chevalier Casentini.

Burton Agnes Hall
A late-Elizabethan house, with a typical façade, designed by the architect Robert Smythson. There are important 18th-century additions and the house contains a noteworthy fine-art collection.

Burton Agnes Manor House
A 17th-century brick façade conceals a Norman undercroft and 15th-century Great Hall, part of the original manor house at Burton Agnes.

Burton Constable Hall
An Elizabethan mansion built onto an earlier brick manor house. Extensive remodelling during the 18th century resulted in a typically Georgian interior throughout much of the Hall.

Cannon Hall
Built in around 1700, with interiors remodelled by Carr of York in the 1760s. Now a museum and art gallery, home to many pieces of fine art.

Carlton Towers
A fine example of Victorian gothic added on to an original 17th century building. Much of the 19th century embellishments were the work of Edward Pugin, son of Augustus Welby Pugin.

Castle Howard
A Baroque palace designed by Sir John Vanbrugh and built in the early 18th century. His designs were never completed and the West Wing was finished in the Palladian style.

Clifford's Tower
The keep of York's medieval castle, constructed in 1244. It is the only example in England of a keep built to a quatrefoil design.

Conisbrough Castle
A Norman castle with a round keep. Built in around 1180 by Hamelin Plantagenet and probably based on his castle in Normandy.

Constable Burton Hall
Built in the style of a Palladian villa, this house was the work of architect John Carr, who came to be known as Carr of York.

Cusworth Park
A Georgian mansion built on a hill overlooking the Don valley. Begun in 1740 by local architect, George Platt, but finished by James Paine.

Duncombe Park
A mansion built in the Baroque style, heavily influenced by Sir John Vanbrugh. The interiors are mainly Victorian, in a French style.

Fairfax House
A magnificent Georgian town house, saved from potential ruin during the 1980s. The interiors are decorated with virtuoso stucco work.

Fountains Abbey
Remains of a great Cistercian monastery, dating from the 12th century. Mostly in ruins but some parts are great examples of early medieval monastic architecture.

Fountains Hall
Mansion built to designs ascribed to Robert Smythson. A fine example of home built in the late Elizabethan style.

Gomersal: Oakwell Hall
A 16th-century Yorkshire yeoman's house with 17th-century decorative details inside. The house was the model for Fieldhead in Charlotte Brontë's Shirley.

Gomersal: Red House
A Georgian house that belonged to wool merchants and manufacturers, the Taylor family. In the 1830s a Mary Taylor became a close friend of Charlotte Brontë.

Halifax: Holdsworth House
The house was begun in the late 16th century and extended in the early 17th. The façade features heavily mullioned windows in an unusual arrangement.

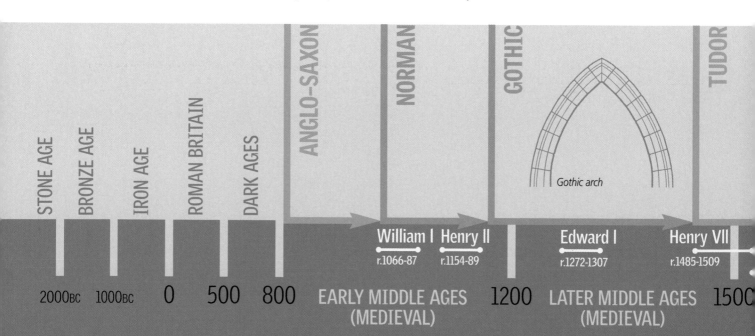

STONE AGE · BRONZE AGE · IRON AGE · ROMAN BRITAIN · DARK AGES · ANGLO–SAXON · NORMAN · GOTHIC · TUDOR

Gothic arch

William I
r.1066-87

Henry II
r.1154-89

Edward I
r.1272-1307

Henry VII
r.1485-1509

2000BC 1000BC 0 500 800 EARLY MIDDLE AGES (MEDIEVAL) 1200 LATER MIDDLE AGES (MEDIEVAL) 1500

Halifax: Shibden Hall
Built in the middle of the 15th century, the house was bought by the Lister family in 1612. It was restored in a Jacobethan style in the early 19th century.

Harewood House
An 18th-century palace, built by Carr of York with magnificent interiors by Robert Adam. Sir Charles Barry made alterations to parts of Harewood in the 19th century.

Haworth: Brontë Parsonage
A simple Georgian house in a moorside village, now maintained as a museum to the Brontë sisters, Charlotte, Emily and Anne.

Hazelwood Castle
A medieval castle with Georgian additions. Much of this later work is believed to have been done by Carr of York.

Helmsley Castle
A castle with ruins dating from throughout the medieval period. An Elizabethan mansion within the walls remains intact.

Hovingham Hall
A Palladian hall built around a riding school and stable complex. The house contains classically inspired interiors and decor.

Huddersfield: Longley Old Hall
Originally believed to be a Jacobean house, much restored in the 19th century. Restoration has revealed a much earlier medieval house within.

Hull: Maister House
A Georgian town house with plain, Palladian style exterior, featuring an Ionic stone doorway. Inside, a grand stone staircase is decorated with stucco work and finished with wrought-iron bannisters.

Hull: Wilberforce House
A brick-built, grand merchant's house, built in the 17th century in a style known as Artisan Mannerist. Some additions were made to the interior during later centuries.

Jorvik Viking Centre
An attraction that centres on archaeological evidence of the Viking settlement at York. Visitors will find reconstructions of Viking homes and shops.

English Baroque

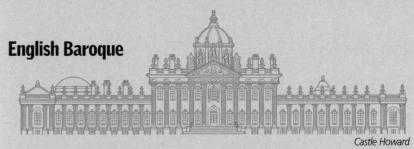

Castle Howard

The Baroque style developed in Italy in the early 17th century, most notably in Rome in the work of Bernini (1598-1680) and Borromini (1599-1667). It was an architectural expression of the Catholic Counter-Reformation, based essentially on Classical proportions but incorporating extravagant curls, scrolls and ovals. Both in structure and decoration, it combined mathematical precision and geometric proportions with sensual, theatrical embellishment.

The style reached Protestant England after the Restoration. Spurred on by the Great Fire of London, Charles II became an enthusiastic builder-monarch, and his lead was emulated by courtiers and continued by later Stuarts (William and Mary, Queen Anne). Christopher Wren and others were commissioned to plan churches, palaces and hospitals with a frenzy not seen since the days of Henry VIII. In English hands, Baroque was less flamboyant than in Europe but equally dramatic, resulting in some of the most splendid architectural set-pieces in the country. Baroque elements can be seen in Wren's St Paul's Cathedral (begun 1675) — most notably in the West façade and the dome. More complete expressions of the style came later, however, in Wren's magnificent Greenwich Hospital, in John Vanbrugh and Nicholas Hawksmoor's Castle Howard, and in Vanbrugh's palace at Blenheim in Oxfordshire.

Keighley: Cliffe Castle
The Victorian mansion of a prosperous mill-owning family, grandly redecorated and refashioned in Parisian style in the late 1800s.

Keighley: East Riddlesden Hall
A Jacobean house partly built in the 1640s, the rest in the 1690s. Only the façade of the later wing remains.

The King's Manor
Once the home to a Benedictine abbey, the Manor was seized by the Crown after the Dissolution. The buildings are mainly medieval with some later additions.

Kiplin Hall
A Jacobean house built in the 1620s. Much of the brickwork outside and the decor inside is Victorian.

Kirkleatham: Turner's Hospital
A monument to local philanthropy, these almshouses were founded in 1676. They were mostly rebuilt in the middle of the 18th century and included a fine Baroque chapel.

Knaresborough: House in the Rock
A picturesque one-off, built during the 18th century into a cleft in the cliffside of a river gorge. Crenellation turned the house into a fort-like structure.

Leeds: Kirkstall Abbey
The ruins of a Cistercian abbey, completed in the late 12th century. The structure of many of the monastic buildings is well preserved.

Lotherton Hall
A Georgian house refashioned in the late 19th century. The interiors are decorated in a variety of different revival styles.

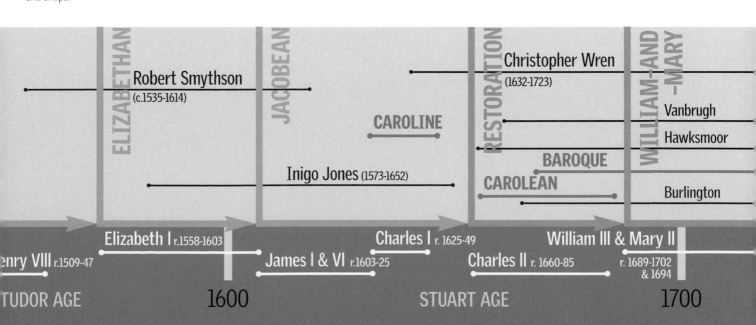

ELIZABETHAN

Robert Smythson (c.1535-1614)

JACOBEAN

Christopher Wren (1632-1723)

RESTORATION

WILLIAM-AND -MARY

CAROLINE

Inigo Jones (1573-1652)

Vanbrugh

Hawksmoor

BAROQUE

CAROLEAN

Burlington

Henry VIII r.1509-47 | Elizabeth I r.1558-1603 | James I & VI r.1603-25 | Charles I r. 1625-49 | Charles II r. 1660-85 | William III & Mary II r. 1689-1702 & 1694

TUDOR AGE | 1600 | STUART AGE | 1700

The cruck frame

The most prominent dwelling of early Anglo-Saxon villages was a 'hall' for the village chief. Fom this evolved one of our earliest architectural forms – the cruck, or inverted V-frame, consisting of two large upright timbers set to curve inward so they joined at the top, braced by a transverse connecting beam. A series of crucks set at intervals, with a ridge beam and rafters laid between them, supported both the roof and sides of a building. The end cruck formed a 'gavel' or gable, and the division of a wall into bays between crucks, with a gable at the end, became the standard style of English building. The number of crucks was a sign of wealth and came to indicate rank – the military chevron had its origin in this inverted V.

   The cruck structure is a uniquely English approach to timber-frame construction. In appearance, it is reminiscent of an upturned boat and some have speculated that it may have been linked to the shipbuilding tradition. Today, the most vivid relics of such early domestic buildings are those that have been rescued and reconstructed in countryside museums, such as Ryedale Folk Museum.

Mansion House, Doncaster
A grand mayoral residence by James Paine, commissioned in 1744. The Rococo plasterwork inside is by Joseph Rose.

Mansion House, York
An early Georgian civic building, possibly by William Etty. The grand interiors match the simple but imposing façade.

Markenfield Hall
A fortified manor house surrounded by a moat and set in farmland. Most of the building dates from early in the 14th century but there were additions and alterations made in the 16th, 18th and 19th centuries.

Marmion Tower
A late 14th-century gateway tower, built for a castle and with a decorative rather than defensive purpose.

Merchant Adventurers' Hall
Part of a group of medieval guild buildings. The Great Hall, with its double nave, sits above an undercroft with a huge four-sided fireplace.

Middleham Castle
Ruins of a medieval castle, originally built on a massive scale. The remains of the fortifications and living areas still give a good idea of what the castle would have looked like.

Middlethorpe Hall
A grand William-and-Mary mansion built with early industrial wealth. Now a hotel, the interiors have been restored.

Moulton Hall
An unusual Jacobean house, built in the 1660s. The façade features three Dutch-style gables. An impressive staircase inside is a perfect example of 'yeoman's baroque'.

Mount Grace Priory: Cell Eight
This medieval 'cell' is in fact a simple two-storey cottage, built for a monk's life of solitary work and contemplation. The living quarters are found on the ground floor, a workroom above.

Newburgh Priory
A house of many parts, the original Augustinian Priory is medieval. Later additions date from the Tudor, Jacobean and Georgian eras.

Newby Hall
A red-bricked William-and-Mary house, built at the end of the 17th century. The building was refashioned in the 18th century by Carr of York and the interiors refurbished by Robert Adam.

Norton Conyers
A 17th-century house with remains of an earlier, 16th-century hall house. The exterior is finished with Dutch-style gables.

Nostell Priory
A Georgian mansion begun in the 1730s by James Paine and finished later in the 18th century by Robert Adam.

Nunnington Hall
The hall dates from the 16th and 17th centuries. The finest feature is the south front, constructed in the 1680s and influenced by French architecture.

Ormesby Hall
A Georgian house with stable block by Carr of York. The interiors are finely decorated and a variety of art is on show.

Richmond Castle
A Norman fortress, the tower keep is well preserved. Some buildings from the 19th-century barracks survive.

Rievaulx Abbey
Ruin of a great Cistercian monastery built in the Early Gothic style. The pointed, typically gothic arches used in the church are among the earliest to be seen in England.

Rievaulx Terrace: Ionic Temple
A small-scale banqueting house, designed in the style of William Kent, who combined Palladian and Baroque influences. It sits at one end of a landscaped terrace, created in the picturesque tradition.

Ripley Castle
A mainly Tudor castle but with a main house built in the 18th century by William Belwood, a follower of Robert Adam.

Ripon: House of Correction
A stern prison, first built in the 17th century and added to in the 19th. Now a museum with examples of prison life to be seen in some cells.

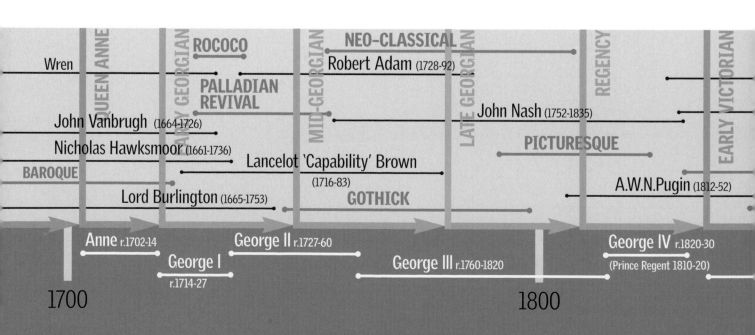

Ripon: Union Workhouse
A Victorian poor house, the casuals' ward remains open as an example of the overnight accommodation vagrants could expect in return for their labour.

Ryedale Folk Museum
A museum that features a collection of domestic buildings, removed from their original settings and reconstructed at Ryedale.

Scampston Hall
A grand Regency mansion, remodelled in the early 1800s by the architect Thomas Leverton. The grounds include a walled garden by Piet Oudolf, which opened in 2004.

Settle: The Folly
An unusual house built in the late 17th century. The windows at the corners of the bays are a particular feature.

Sewerby Hall
A Georgian house, built early in the 1700s with corner bows added in 1808. It is covered in rendering with the windows and other details picked out in stone.

Shandy Hall
A red-brick house much altered and adapted in the late 18th century by its most famous resident, Laurence Sterne.

Sheffield: Bishop's House
A 15th-century house; the ground floor is stone, the structure above is half timbered. The building was extended in the 17th century. It is now a museum.

Sion Hill Hall
Built in 1913 by Walter Brierley of York, known as the 'Lutyens of the North', this is a low red-brick house with steep roof and tall chimneys.

Skipton Castle
A fine example of a medieval castle with seven towers. Inside is a courtyard known as Conduit Court.

Sledmere House
The original house was built in the late 18th century, but a fire in 1911 destroyed all but the outer walls. The Georgian interiors, mainly by Joseph Rose, were fully restored.

St William's College
A group of medieval buildings, put up in around 1450 as accommodation for the priests of York Minster, much altered and adapted over the years.

Stockeld Park
Georgian house by James Paine, with later Victorian addition. Considered by Pevsner to be an example of a Vanbrughian revival.

Sutton Park
Mid-18th-century house, believed to be the work of Thomas Atkinson. A plain exterior, topped with a wide pediment and flanked by two wings.

Swinton Park
A house much changed and added to over the years, mainly during the 19th century A tower and crenellations give the house a fortified look.

Temple Newsam
A Jacobean palace built around three sides of a courtyard. Most of the interiors are Jacobean reproduction or revival; some are Georgian.

Thirsk: James Herriot's House
A Georgian town house, once the home of Alf Wight, creator of James Herriot. The rooms have been restored to their 1950s furnishings and decor.

Treasurer's House
A Jacobean house built on the site of earlier residences. Restored in the Edwardian era by Frank Greene to his taste and ideas.

Wakefield: Clarke Hall
A brick-built, E-plan Jacobean house with fragments of an older hall remaining. Inside, rooms are furnished as replicas of 17th-century interiors.

Wentworth Castle
A palatial house with three main façades. The original house was built in 1670, further additions in Baroque and Palladian styles were made in the 18th century.

Wentworth Woodhouse
An 18th-century palace set in parkland. The front is 19 bays long. The massive central entrance portico is reached by a double flight of steps.

John Carr of York

John Carr (1723–1807) was one of the most successful and best-known architects of his day. The pinnacle of his career was Harewood House, a collaboration with Robert Adam. A mark of his fame was recognition by the London Architects Club who invited him to become a member, a rare distinction for a provincial architect.

John Carr was born in the village of Horbury near Wakefield, the son of a quarry owner and mason, Robert Carr. He was quick to learn the masons art from his father, and by 1750 was constructing the designs of architects such as Lord Burlington, a champion of the Palladian revival. His big break as an architect came in 1754, when his design was selected for a new grandstand at Knavesmere. This brought him into contact with other potential clients, and his reputation for reliability and quality made him a popular choice among the gentry.

In addition to grand domestic architecture, his works included public buildings, churches and bridges. He was made a freeman of the city of York in 1757 and his portrait, by Sir William Beechy, hangs in York's Mansion House.

Whitby Banqueting House
Remains of a splendid banqueting house built in the 1670s. Now modernized and used as the visitor centre for Whitby Abbey.

York Castle Museum
Once York's city jail, built in the 18th century. Carr of York was responsible for one wing and some exercise yards. Today, it is home to 'historic lifestyle' displays.

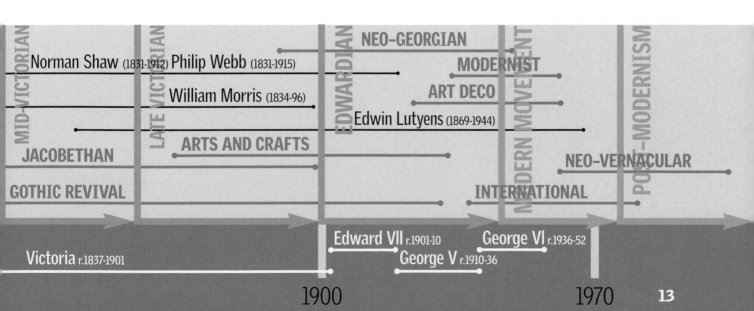

MID-VICTORIAN

LATE VICTORIAN

EDWARDIAN

NEO-GEORGIAN

MODERNIST

ART DECO

MODERN MOVEMENT

POST-MODERNISM

Norman Shaw (1831-1912) Philip Webb (1831-1915)

William Morris (1834-96)

Edwin Lutyens (1869-1944)

ARTS AND CRAFTS

JACOBETHAN

NEO-VERNACULAR

GOTHIC REVIVAL

INTERNATIONAL

Edward VII r.1901-10

George VI r.1936-52

George V r.1910-36

Victoria r.1837-1901

1900

1970

East

Sledmere House

East Riding

Riding

Burton Agnes hall

★ ★ ★ ★ ☆ Late-Elizabethan house by Robert Smythson

At Burton Agnes, 7 miles SW of Bridlington; private house and garden, open part year

I first saw Burton Agnes with a low evening sun warming its brick crevices and deepening the shadows of the yews across the lawn. It is the perfect English house, embodying the climax of the first great age of domestic architecture, Elizabethan, at the hand of Robert Smythson, its finest exponent. The house was begun in 1601 by Sir Henry Griffith, descendant of the Norman owner of the estate, Roger de Stuteville. Burton Agnes has been held in line of descent by Griffiths, Boyntons and Cunliffe-Listers ever since, now as a trust.

The house has no great park but is reached up steps direct from the village. The entrance is through a three-storey gatehouse of 1610. This is of pink bricks and has domed turrets. Renaissance features include arched niches on the ground floor and a stone frontispiece flanked by caryatids. The front courtyard is now a lawn populated by clipped topiary yews. The façade is a typical Smythson stage-set, a sequence of projecting and receding bays, some squared, some bowed. There is no obvious door, the entrance being tucked in beside one of the bays, yet with a frontispiece of its own. This is in the same manner as at Chastleton (Oxfordshire), suggesting some Smythson link with the latter house – or at least an enthusiastic imitator.

'It is the perfect English house'

The Great Hall is without parallel of any house of this period. Where the Italians played with space, the English played with ornament. The screen and chimneypiece at Burton Agnes fight each other to a draw. The former rises the full height of the entrance wall. Three tiers of tableaux form a gallery of sculpted figures. Set in an architectural frame, they are a Jacobean Elgin Marbles. The chimneypiece replies in alabaster, Wise and Foolish Virgins supporting a celebration of the Griffith, then Boynton, line of owners. It is flanked by large portraits of 18th-century Griffith Boyntons.

The doorway to the inner hall is a work of art in itself. Here stands a Nonsuch chest, its decoration recalling Henry VIII's lost palace in Surrey, and a Gheeraerts painting of the three daughters of the original house. The drawing room beyond is a glowing chamber, ranking in spectacle with the hall. It is covered in panelling with painted arches and stumpy pilasters.

The house now changes key to Georgian. In the 18th-century Chinese Room, cool walls frame lacquer panels depicting Chinese festivals. The dining room is enlivened by a fireplace brought down from the Long Gallery and is hung with landscapes by William Marlow and Thomas Gainsborough, and portraits by Sir Joshua Reynolds and Francis Cotes.

Below left The Drawing room is home to another piece of virtuoso Elizabethan carving. On a panel above the fireplace, a Dance of Death is acted out. A skeleton triumphs over worldly vanities and divides the Just and Unjust between Heaven and Hell. **Below right** In the Queen's room, realistic-looking honeysuckle plasterwork twines across the ceiling, and patterns of leaves and flowers run above the panelling. The 18th-century bed was originally in Sewerby Hall (page 27).

The staircase is a funnel of grandeur. Wide, shallow treads seem compressed into a central well, as if a farthingale were trying to negotiate a corkscrew. The craftsman has carried the flights upwards using a group of four newel posts on small arches. The big first floor drawing room, panelled *c*1700, is light and classical, its furniture copied from Kent, Adam and Chippendale. French Post-Impressionists hang on the walls. Burton Agnes never ceases to surprise.

The state bedrooms are predictably sumptuous. The King's Room has exquisite panelling and scrollwork on the bed-head, the centre of which is covered in original sky-blue damask. The Queen's Room has a plasterwork ceiling of honeysuckle so deeply sculpted it seems ready to creep down the walls and wind itself round the furniture. It was once haunted by a daughter of the house who, on her deathbed,

demanded her head be buried within the walls of Burton Agnes. It was not, and she duly wandered the place so determinedly that she had to be exhumed and accorded her wish.

The crowning glory of Burton Agnes is the Long Gallery, running the entire length of the top floor. This is no Elizabethan attic but a true gallery, again similar to that at Chastleton. The room was later divided and most of the ceiling lost. The barrel vault was restored and replicated by Francis Johnson first in 1951 and the remainder in 1974. Its peach-coloured walls with white pilasters are hung with works by Courbet, Cézanne, Corot, Boudin, Gauguin, Matisse, Renoir, Rouault and Pissarro.

This splendid collection was mostly gathered by Marcus Wickham-Boynton, who died in 1989. Burton Agnes still has an 'artist in residence', resident in what is already a work of art.

'Burton Agnes still has an "artist in residence

Below The Long Gallery is the perfect setting for some of Burton Agnes Hall's finest treasures. Among the works on display are some modern, commissioned pieces. These include a tapestry by Kaffe Fassett, embroidery by Janet Haigh, and furniture by John Makepeace. His gallery seat, in the middle of the room, was inspired by patterns in the restored ceiling and includes colours taken from the paintings on the walls.

esident in what is already **a work of art.'**

Above On the ground floor of the original manor house at Burton Agnes is this grand lower chamber that has somehow survived the passing of the centuries. The vaulted ceiling with chamfered ribs, and the heavy round pillars that support it, are typical of Norman architecture.

Burton Agnes manor house

⭐ Manor house with Norman undercroft and medieval great hall

At Burton Agnes, 7 miles SW of Bridlington; English Heritage, open part year

Sitting outside the formal walls of Burton Agnes Hall, the manor house pre-dates that house by four centuries. The outside is of brick and with 18th-century windows, but this is a façade. The building was the Great Hall of the original Griffith manor, and was built by the present family's predecessor, Roger de Stuteville, in about 1173. Presumably respect for ancestors protected it down the years; it is now guarded by English Heritage. Even its conversion for use as a Georgian laundry was deferential.

The entrance leads into the undercroft. This is exceptionally grand and well preserved. The massive piers have waterleaf capitals and the vaults are heavily ribbed. Upstairs is the hall itself, much altered but still with an appropriate sense of majesty. The roof has a kingpost and dates from the 15th century. Original fragments can be detected in the walling and a small slit window survives, lighting the staircase. I overheard a tourist who had just visited the big house next door saying, 'I prefer this one: I know what I could do with it.'

Burton Constable hall

★ ★ ★ ☆ An Elizabethan mansion converted into a Grand Tour treasure trove

At Skirlaugh, 8 miles NE of Hull; private house and grounds, open part year

Burton Constable invites comparison with its near namesake, Burton Agnes. It is contemporary but in every way different. Both were Elizabethan creations by old Yorkshire families whose descendants still occupy them. Burton Constable, though the bigger, was not big enough for the 18th-century William Constable, whose character and taste dominate the house. He expanded and Georgianized the interior, making it unmanageable for the 21st century. The house now has an air of mild desperation. Where Burton Agnes Hall is compact and intimate, Burton Constable seems lonely and lost in the open fields of Holderness.

Constables still live in one wing. The rest is run by a trust and, greatly to its credit, by the City of Leeds which owns the contents of the main part of the house. Work needs doing, although much of the charm lies in how much is still undone. This is one of the few large houses whose nether regions remain undiscovered and uncatalogued. Even my guide seemed lost among unlit storerooms, passages, basements and turrets. This is a place of secrets and hermits. Long may it remain so.

Sir John Constable, of Norman descent, built a new front onto his Burton property in the 1560s, forming an Elizabethan façade with a central bay window and side entrance to a screens passage. William Constable's 18th-century alterations left little of this work untouched. He installed the present central door and frontispiece (below), rising to the Constable coat of arms on the roof. The resulting façade seems rather flat. The front door leads directly into the Great Hall, bringing with it wind and rain and demonstrating the virtues of screens passages. The Hall of 1763 is by Timothy Lightoler, deeply coved with mini-vaults above a heavy cornice. It is a remarkable example of a Jacobean revival interior, well before its time.

William Constable was a man of divided loyalties. He was reputedly sorry to part with the Elizabethan Great Hall and screen, in which he liked to dine, medieval fashion, with his wife and thirty-four servants, his 'family' as he called them. Yet he was also an assiduous Grand

Above The main fireplace in the Long Gallery was created in scagliola by Domenico Bartoli, in around 1765. Just below the mantel is a panel depicting an idealized view of ruined antiquity. **Below** The cantilevered Grand Staircase was designed by Timothy Lightoler in the 1760s. The original fittings for candles are still set along the handrail.

Tourist and longed for a house that reflected the new Augustan taste. Demosthenes and Hercules flank the fireplace, Marcus Aurelius and Sappho are on the mantelshelf. The Constable arms on the chimneypiece are attended by boughs of imitation oak and laurel. Huge family portraits stare down from the walls, including one of William and his wife in ancient Roman garb. This was truly a man torn between past and future.

William apparently rejected plans for an adjacent dining room by Robert Adam in favour of one by Lightoler. Here the Middle Ages altogether vanish. Three giant medallions decorate the walls, one showing the Three Graces dancing before Pan, another Bacchus and Ariadne. William, in a fervour of indecision about whom to prefer, employed different craftsmen on each feature of the room. The ceiling, copied from Italy, is by Joseph Cortese. Attention was paid to every detail, from the grapes on the overmantel to the crests on the wine glasses. Nothing was less 'provincial' than the taste of these Yorkshire grandees.

The Grand Staircase occupies a large volume in the centre of the house. Pevsner regarded it as 'uneventful' but he did not see the fierce yellow paint applied to it in 1972. This out-dazzles even the heavy-duty pictures intended to fill the open wallspace. Coriolanus's mother glares across the emptiness at Constable forebears, the Astons.

The staircase balcony leads into the Long Gallery, which runs the length of the rear elevation. This is in the form of a richly panelled library, with ceiling of roundels and pendants, again Jacobean revival. It has a charming Georgian fireplace with flanking columns garlanded with flowers growing from pots. Embroidered samplers and 17th-century chairs mix with Nanking vases and early portraits.

We now see another side to William Constable. He was not just a Grand Tourist but a scientist and collector. Closets and 'cabinets of curiosities' follow one after another, filled with a phenomenal variety of objects – guns, fossils, shells and scientific instruments. These include an early electricity machine, a condenser and a table pump. Georgian science laboratory co-existed with drawing room. Burton Constable is the best example of an Enlightened gentleman's collection.

The bedrooms are also Georgian. The Gold Bedroom has a Rococo four-poster and exotically framed mirrors. A suite of state rooms was converted from the old Tudor Great Chamber and from what may have started as a pele tower buried in the later building. The conversion demonstrates Lightoler at his most inventive.

Burton Constable now delightfully loses control. Rooms fall out of each other apparently at random. On the ground floor is a Catholic chapel, in the richest of Italianate decoration of 1844 and still in use. The adjacent silk-hung ballroom was designed in 1775 by James Wyatt and furnished by Chippendale. The door handles are of Worcester porcelain.

Three more drawing rooms follow, by which stage the visitor's head is whirling. In the Chippendale Room is a mechanical orange tree with singing birds. The Chinese Room has wallpaper as good as any I know, each wall a sweeping composition of birds fluttering across leaves and flowers. The room is littered with oriental figures and the chandelier is a large Chinese lantern. There are gilded dragons everywhere. This is a miniature Brighton Pavilion of the North.

Despite evidence of the presence of some London craftsmen, most of Burton Constable was by workers from Hull and Doncaster. It demonstrates not just the taste of one country gentleman in the Georgian era but the quality of work generally present in the North of England at the time.

Below William Constable, who owned Burton Constable from 1747 until his death in 1791, was a voracious collector. He was fascinated by science and natural history and the contents of his 'cabinet of curiosities' reflects these interests. Most of the items were gathered together during the middle years of the 18th century and include such 'natural curiosities' as a rhinoceros horn, dried or stuffed fish and reptiles, sawfish saws, shark jaws and swordfish swords.

Maister house

★ Georgian merchant's house with inspiring stucco staircase

160 High Street, Hull; National Trust, stairwell accessible to public view

The Maister family were prosperous Hull merchants with a business and house in the High Street. One April night in 1743 a fire consumed the building, killing Henry Maister's wife, daughter and two servants. He himself survived another eighteen months but his brother took charge of the rebuilding. The exterior was severe and Palladian. The interior, or at least one feature of it, was astonishing. The staircase of the Maister House is virtuoso plasterwork. Although the building is used as offices, it is owned by the National Trust and the stairwell is accessible to view.

Work on the staircase involved consultation with none other than Lord Burlington. Why he should have concerned himself with a merchant's house in Hull is unclear, except that he had property in the East Riding and would have known many local citizens.

The ground floor would have been occupied by business, so a grand entrance to the family chambers above was important. The stairs, which rise the full height of the interior, were decorated by a local stuccoist, Joseph Page, with a wrought-iron balustrade by Robert Bakewell of Derby.

Page's stucco work is superb. Swags, busts, statue niches and medallions adorn the walls. The first-floor landing has palatial doors and swirling Rococo decoration in the ceiling panels. Roses fill the undersides of the top gallery, above which rises a Rococo ceiling to the top-lit lantern. It is as rich as could be, buried within a Hull office block.

Below Legend has it that Henry Maister insisted on a stone staircase with iron balustrades and plaster decoration when he rebuilt his house because his wife and daughter had been unable to escape when the original wooden stairs were destroyed by the fire of 1743. Classically inspired busts and statues adorn the walls of the stairwell. The statue of Ceres (right), the Roman mother-earth goddess, is believed to be the work of Sir Henry Cheere.

'Oh, to have known **Hull** in the **17th century!**'

Wilberforce house

⭐⭐ Birthplace of the pioneering anti-slavery campaigner

25 High Street, Hull; local authority museum, open all year

Oh, to have known Hull in the 17th century! Grand merchants' houses backed onto gardens and staithes, at the end of which ships from across the North Sea and Baltic dropped anchor. Every house was a family home, a business and a travel agency in one. The nearest extant example I have found is at Old Cochin in Kerala, India, but Hull was grander.

One such house would have been the home of a Baltic trader, Robert Wilberforce. His son William, born here in 1759, was to be the great slave-trade abolitionist. The house was designed almost a century earlier by William Catlyn, a Hull bricklayer of ability and learning, who also

William Wilberforce
1759-1833

William Wilberforce, shown here in a portrait on display at the Wilberforce House museum, became Hull's MP in 1780, aged just 21. He was involved in the anti-slavery movement from 1788, leading the campaign in the House of Commons. After a 19-year struggle, he saw the slave trade declared illegal in 1807, but it was not until a month after his death, in 1833, that slavery itself was abolished across the British Empire.

designed neighbouring Crowle House. He crammed his learning into the façade. The mid-17th century style was known as Artisan Mannerist, emanating in part from the Netherlands.

The frontage to the High Street is of nine bays, which is very wide. The façade is entirely of brick with fake rustication and pilasters on the first floor. Most odd is the frontispiece over the door. This rises three storeys with no parapet or gable but flanking pilasters, with each rusticated panel adorned with a 'jewel'. Pedimental niches flank the doorway arch.

Although the interior of the house is now the Wilberforce Museum, many original features survive. The drawing room downstairs was refashioned in the 18th century with Ionic pilasters and a Rococo ceiling. The fine staircase with Rococo plasterwork is spoiled with over-clever painting. The medallions are bright blue and the Wilberforce eagle black.

On the first floor, the Banqueting Room has excellent panelling, especially round the fireplace, and a treasure chest. Most of the other rooms suffer from museumitis and political correctness. Hull citizens apparently still need telling that slavery was not a good idea.

Left Some parts of Wilberforce House have changed little since the 17th century. One of the bedrooms retains the original panelling that lined the walls and the blue-and-white Dutch tiles inside the fireplace. To the right of the chimney breast is a dummy board. This kind of cut-out figure is thought to have been used as a fire guard, protecting the room's occupants from the fiercer flames.

Sewerby hall

⭐ Georgian house set in Victorian gardens

At Sewerby, 2 miles NE of Bridlington;
local authority museum – house open
part year, gardens open all year

Sewerby Hall was the seat of the Greame
family from 1694. They were local land
agents but pretended descent from the Scots
Grahams, Dukes of Montrose. A Victorian
Greame, called 'Yarborough', so preferred his
Christian name as to change his surname,
becoming Yarborough Yarborough.

Those days are past. Few houses are sadder than those overlain with an alternative use
for which they were not designed. Sewerby was sold to the local council in the 1930s and
has become a museum, looking out to sea from a stately terrace and weeping for its past.
Its magnificent garden is defaced by health-and-safety cages which protect the public from
the municipal llamas.

The house remains a fine one, built in the early 18th century and covered in cream render
with stone window dressings. The corner bows were added in 1808. The interior rooms not
filled with museum cases have good panelling and plasterwork. Fluted pilasters flank the arch
from the hall to the cantilevered staircase. The best room is the early Georgian Oak Room.
It retains dark panelling and a shell-headed niche, decoration repeated in the bedroom above.

Sewerby has been refurnished and an effort made to recapture some of its past charm.
One room is dedicated to Amy Johnson, the early aviator. Yarborough's Victorian gardens are
exotic, including one of the oldest monkey puzzle trees in England.

Amy Johnson
1903–41

Born in Hull on 1st July 1903, local herione Amy Johnson
became known as the 'Queen of the Air'. She qualified as a
pilot in 1929 and in 1930 made the first of many record-
breaking attempts, becoming the first woman to fly solo to
Australia. During World War II, Johnson joined the Air
Transport Auxiliary, responsible for ferrying planes to
airfields. It was on a mission for the ATA in January 1941
that she bailed out over the Thames estuary and drowned.

Sledmere house

★★★ Restored Georgian house with re-created Joseph Rose interiors

At Sledmere, 8 miles NW of Driffield; private house and grounds, open part year

Sledmere is a Yorkshire Lanhydrock (Cornwall), a house destroyed by fire (in 1911) and reinstated to the enhanced standards of Edwardian country-house living. Here the reproduction is Georgian rather than Jacobean. The house was the seat of the Sykes family of Hull, grandees of the East Riding. It was begun in the mid-18th century but mostly designed, largely by Sir Christopher Sykes, in the 1780s. His passion for tripartite windows, each set within an arch, lends the place a noble eccentricity. The outstanding plasterwork was by Joseph Rose. Even if the post-fire interiors seem indisputably 20th century, the reproduction of Rose's work is a wonder of conservation. So too are the post-war amendments by Francis Johnson. Sledmere is, in truth, a 'Georgian' house designed over three centuries.

The small entrance hall is adorned with weapons, trophies and a rusticated fireplace. A statue of Laocoon was relieved of pomposity (on my visit) by a bowler hat. Beyond is the central hall, created by Walter Brierley after the 1911 fire, as the spine and chief adornment of Sledmere. It runs across almost the entire building. Scagliola columns the colour of amber divide the hall into bays adorned with Adamish swags and scrolls on soft green walls. The stairs that form the climax are Baroque in effect. They narrow past large urns before dividing in front of a copy of the Apollo Belvedere and turning back to the landing. This is a splendid space, the more dramatic when an organ under the stairs is playing full blast during public visits. Music is a feature of Sledmere.

Right Brightly coloured and patterned tiles, so typical of those used in Islamic architecture, were specially made in Damascus for the Turkish Room at Sledmere. The room's interior is a copy of one of the sultan's apartments in the Yeni Mosque in Istanbul and was created for Sir Mark Sykes, the 6th Baronet, by the Armenian artist, David Ohanessian.

The reception rooms downstairs are lavishly decorated. The relief plasterwork in the music room is after Adam. In front of another organ is an exquisite Chinese enamel table. The drawing room is a celebration of Joseph Rose. His ceiling in the Adam style depicts 'Greek religious rites' amid a familiar decoration of shells, anthemion and laurel. The walls are hung with Sykes portraits, including one of Sir Tatton Sykes on horseback, the embodiment of a great Victorian 'improver'. The boudoir has scarlet damask walls with another Adam-style ceiling and marquetry chests. The dining room is in blue and gold with a Romney of Sir Christopher Sykes, builder of the house, an English country gentleman and his wife.

The glory of Sledmere is upstairs: Sir Christopher's great library was restored to Rose's original designs and colours by Francis Johnson in 1979–81. As a work of architectural reinstatement, it ranks with that of Uppark (Sussex). The ceiling is arched and vaulted in the richest of Roman motifs, gold and blue on a cream background. A marquetry floor repeats the old carpet, lost in the fire. The original book collection included a Gutenberg Bible. Mercifully it had been sold before the fire and is now in New York's Metropolitan Museum.

On the way out, visitors can see the Turkish Room, copied from a sultan's apartment in Istanbul. It is a dazzling display of blue tiles. The park is by Capability Brown.

North Y

Oliver's Ducket, Aske Hall

North Yorkshire

Yorkshire

Aske hall

★ ★ Aristocratic Georgian mansion in an ornamental park

2 miles N of Richmond; private house, tours available by appointment

The seat of the Marquesses of Zetland broods on its hillside outside Richmond, pondering a future of corporate activity and rural enterprise. Can an old lady dabble in such things and keep her dignity? The house seen from the main road is magnificently framed by trees. It was much reduced in the 1960s by the neo-classicist, Claud Phillimore, who refaced the main façade in stone. In the 1990s, the entrance was placed at the back, in a quiet courtyard behind the wall of a medieval pele tower, a rare survival in Yorkshire.

The principal reception rooms flank the main hall behind the portico. They are mostly devoted to the Zetland picture collection. In the hall, dark Stuart courtiers gaze out from beetle brows. The marble fireplace is a relic from the sadly demolished Clumber Park in Nottinghamshire. Richard Wilson landscapes illuminate the saloon. The drawing room, possibly by Carr of York, has a Zoffany of a room in a family's house in London, showing a row of bronze statues on the mantelpiece, which the present family has enterprisingly tried to reassemble after an earlier sale.

The approach to the house is past gargantuan Victorian stables more magnificent than the house itself. In the grounds at Aske is a fragment of Richmond Castle, demolished and rebuilt as a folly called Oliver's Ducket (below).

5 miles NE of Skipton; privately owned, exterior can be viewed

The ruin of Barden Tower stands in the valley of the Wharfe above Bolton Abbey, where the gorge broadens onto the moor. It was one of many Pennine houses taken over by Lady Anne Clifford, a Royalist whose response to Cromwell was to restore the ancient homes of her ancestors. The tower had been a feudal base for resisting Scottish raids down Wharfedale. In the 14th century it passed to the Cliffords of Skipton. Henry Clifford had been sent to live with shepherds as a youth, to protect him from the Wars of the Roses. Known as the 'Shepherd Lord', he resided at the pele tower of Barden under Henry VII, regarding it as safer than his place at Skipton.

Clifford rebuilt Barden but it was his descendant, Lady Anne, who restored what had become a ruin. Although her ownership was contested by Lady Burlington of adjacent Bolton Abbey, Anne brooked no opposition. She restored every property she claimed, journeying between them in a litter. She added chapels and almshouses where she could. After her death in 1676, Barden reverted to the Burlington family, through whom it descended to the Dukes of Devonshire, who own it still.

Lady Anne is probably responsible for the fine arched entrance to Barden and the flanking windows with Jacobean tracery. The main façade is symmetrical, with tower wings rising four storeys. The domestic rooms are on one side and services on the other. Although now roofless, the walls are intact and form an impressive example of the domestic buildings that Lady Anne sought to maintain, with appropriate ritual, against the Cromwellian revolution.

To the south of the house, a 17th-century chapel and priest's house form a picturesque foreground to the sombre ruin next door.

Barden tower

Beningbrough hall

★★★★☆ A Grand-Tour house with pictures on loan from the National Portrait Gallery

At Beningbrough, 8 miles NW of York; National Trust, open part year

The young John Bourchier returned home from the Grand Tour and Italy in 1706 and married his wealthy childhood sweetheart, Mary Bellwood. Their new house at Beningbrough was designed by a local man, William Thornton. It was to be based on Bourchier's researches in Rome, with occasional flourishes of Borromini and Bernini on the entrance front. The house descended through Earles and Dawnays before being acquired by Lord Chesterfield in 1917. It passed to the National Trust in 1957.

The façades are in red brick and look back to the 17th century rather than forward to the Palladians. The entrance leads directly into the hall, a huge chamber which defies the simplicity of the exterior. Giant pilasters soar two storeys to groined vaults. They pass balconied openings from the staircases, in the manner of Vanbrugh. Portraits by Sir Godfrey Kneller look down with satisfaction from the walls.

The plan is old-fashioned, with state bedrooms on the ground floor, still with their closets. The resulting enfilade of panelled rooms is more Dutch than Italian in style. Decoration is wood rather than plaster and the walls carry tapestries, china and miniatures.

Above Beningbrough is entered through a grand double-height hall, a magnificent example of English Baroque. Openings in the walls at the upper level are furnished with balustrades. These interior balconies were an ideal vantage point, no doubt, from which to observe comings and goings in the hall. The observer is also framed by the opening to become, for a moment, a living portrait among the other pictures.

Doors stand open wide between linked rooms on the ground floor at Beningbrough. Looking from the State Dressing Room, as here, the eye is drawn through each doorway in turn. The receding squares and rectangles formed by door and picture frames, wood panels and cast shadows, combine to create a classic vista, a view reminiscent, perhaps, of Dutch interior paintings of the 17th century.

Left This magnificent state bed found its home at Beningbrough in the early 20th century when it was installed in the State Bedchamber by Lord Chesterfield after he bought the Hall. Hung with rich damask, it soars above the other furniture in the room.

The prize of Beningbrough is Lord Chesterfield's state bed. Brought by him from Holme Lacy (Herefordshire), it is French in style and heavy with red damask.

The adjacent dining room is hung with Kneller's portraits of members of the Kit-Cat Club, borrowed from the National Portrait Gallery. This group of Whig literati pledged themselves to maintain the Protestant succession when it was considered at risk under Queen Anne. The faces are so stylized as to reveal little individual personality.

The drawing room has woodcarving worthy of Grinling Gibbons and the enfilade is completed by a dressing room and closet, the latter with parts of a Chinese screen set into the panelling, matching the Chinese lacquerwork furniture. On every wall there seems to be Kneller, as if he worked exclusively for this one house.

The climb to the saloon reveals glimpses of the upper level of the hall through openings and balconies. On the first floor, corridors penetrate the house from end to end. The saloon is light yet grand, with Bourchier more in Italian mode. Pilasters are gilded and ceilings coffered. In the attic are more paintings lent to the house by the National Portrait Gallery, an admirable practice.

Bolton castle

★ ★ ☆ Medieval keep-castle overlooking Wensleydale, once prison to Mary, Queen of Scots

At Castle Bolton, 5 miles W of Leyburn; private house and grounds, open part year

Bolton is a 14th-century fortress palace. Held by descendants of the 12th-century Scropes, it is everything English Heritage castles are not allowed to be. It is damp, smelly, rambling, romantic and faintly desperate. The stones do not speak for themselves but are helped in the task. A waxen Mary Queen of Scots sits huddling with her retinue in a cold bedchamber. A priest mumbles his vespers in a dripping chapel. A horse tries to grind corn on a threshing floor and I distinctly heard a man groaning in the dungeon.

The castle was built and crenellated in 1379 by the 1st Baron, Richard Scrope, and completed by his son, William. The latter went on to acquire the Kingdom of the Isle of Man and serve as Treasurer to Richard II. For this, he was beheaded without trial, first of a series of mishaps to befall the Scropes. The line survived through illegitimate heirs. The castle incarcerated Mary, Queen of Scots in 1568, on her way to Fotheringay,

but was slighted by Cromwell after declaring for the King in the Civil War. In 1653, a Scrope daughter married a Powlett, who became Duke of Bolton and moved from the Castle into Bolton Hall. Orde-Powlett descendants continue as owners and custodians.

Restoration of the old castle began in the 1990s and continues today. Unlike Skipton's informal range of buildings round a courtyard (see page 102), Bolton is a single rectangular fortress, one of the finest to survive in this form in the country, with square corner towers five storeys high. To Pevsner, Bolton represented a 'balance between the claims of defence, domestic complexity and comfort, and an aesthetically considered orderliness'.

The castle looks out onto Wensleydale as if still its overlord. The entrance, in summer, is through the double gatehouse, a narrow passage where arrows, pitch, boiling oil and other missiles could be rained down on attackers. Inside, the courtyard is cobbled, the massive walls and towers looming on all sides. The ground floor chambers were for stabling, storage and food preparation. All are in good repair.

Though the outer walls and lower floors survive, only the south-west tower remains complete to its roof. The west range of the castle and the tower rooms are well restored, the latter with solar and two floors of bedchambers above. The nursery room retains its original ceiling. The interiors are roughly furnished as they might have been during Mary, Queen of Scots' stay. We can see where water jugs would have rested by latrines, where fires would have burned and salt kept dry.

The grander rooms are along the west range, essentially the private apartments leading at right angles to the now ruined Great Hall. These comprise the Guest Hall on the first floor and the Great Chamber above. Valiant efforts have been made to find carpets, tapestries, arms and banners to bring these rooms to life. It might be better to concentrate on recreating just one. A human bone was recently found still manacled to a rock in the dungeon.

At Warthill, 5 miles NE of York; private house, open part year and by appointment for remainder

Brockfield Hall was built for Benjamin Agar, lord of the manors of Stockton on Forest and Holtby. The Agars owned the Hall until it was sold in 1923. In 1951 it became the family home of the late Lord Martin Fitzalan Howard and his wife; today, it is the home of their daughter and her family. Lord Howard was a younger brother of the late Duke of Norfolk and son of the late Baroness Beaumont of Carlton Towers (see page 42). Brockfield Hall is still hung with interesting portraits of the Baroness's influential old Roman Catholic family, the Stapletons.

The house is restrained and domestic, indeed it might be a country rectory. The design, of 1804, was by Peter Atkinson, whose father had been assistant to the famous Carr of York. By the beginning of the 19th century, Atkinson had become York's leading architect. Brockfield's chief feature is the entrance hall and staircase. Their curved walls fill the heart of the house, the stairs circling upwards to a balcony whose Venetian window towers over the front door.

The other reception rooms have dignified Regency interiors. The oval drawing room has a caryatid fireplace surround and delicate plaster ceiling. A case contains a collection of unusual glass walking sticks.

Above The entrance at Brockfield leads into an impressive oval hall. A cantilevered stone staircase rises up around the curved walls, and the steps pause briefly at a small half landing allowing a view from the spectacular Venetian window.

Brockfield hall

Broughton hall

Right The conservatory at Broughton is a fine example of glasshouse architecture. Metalwork, stone and glass combine to create a light and elegant structure. From the stunning displays of hot-house plants, the eye is lead out towards the Italianate gardens beyond.

✦ ✦ ✧ Georgian house with Italianate grounds and private chapel

At Broughton, 3 miles W of Skipton; private house and grounds, tours available by appointment

The Tempests were staunch recusants who can trace their line back to the 12th century. They show no sign of dying out. The younger generation draw cartoons for *Country Life* and run an enterprise consultancy in the basement. The stables are the Broughton Hall Business Park with a dozen company name-plates on the gatepost.

The Georgian house of *c*1750 has been much extended. William Atkinson added wings in 1810. George Webster of Kendal added a clock-tower to the stables and a monumental *porte-cochère* to the main front in 1839. The effect is in keeping with the Italianate gardens to the left and behind. Broughton has panache.

The interior turns on a handsome central hall with scagliola columns. This leads straight through the house to an 1850s conservatory beyond, forming a happy vista to W. A. Nesfield's Italianate gardens climbing the hillside at the back. The conservatory wall has a mural of various past Tempest homes, including one in Africa.

The reception rooms are by William Atkinson, Regency and enjoyably ponderous. The Red Drawing Room has an Egyptian fireplace and is hung with copies of Old Masters once in the family's possession, a relief from the relentless portraiture that dominates so many lesser English houses. The library seems entombed in leather, with a ceiling of oak leaves and posies.

The house is very much occupied and the Gothic private chapel very much worshipped in. Its Edwardian stencil work recalls that at Madresfield Court (Worcestershire). Tridentine Mass is held here four times a week, as it has since time immemorial.

Carlton towers

⭐ ⭐ A Victorian Gothic extravaganza

At Carlton, 6 miles S of Selby; private house and grounds, viewing by arrangement

From a distance, we see only the black towers and turrets of a fantastic architectural joke. The Manor of Carlton was owned by Stapletons since the Norman Conquest. They were grand-daughters of Bess of Hardwick and, as Catholic Beaumonts, founded Beaumont College.

In 1869, the young Henry Stapleton, Lord Beaumont, renounced his father's conversion to Anglicanism, reverted to Catholicism and decided to rebuild the family home in an effusive neo-medieval style. No sooner was this under way than Beaumont left to fight variously for the Spanish pretender, Don Carlos, and in the Franco-Prussian and Zulu wars. He returned, became a Kensington property speculator and died a ruined man.

Beaumont's architect at Carlton was Edward Pugin, son of Augustus Welby, who had worked on a similarly eccentric project at Catholic Scarisbrick Hall (Lancashire). According to Mark Girouard, Edward had 'an uncontrollable temper, a passion for rows and litigation and a complete lack of prudence … In his buildings as in his quarrels, he never knew when to stop.' The original house was 17th century, extended in the 18th and 19th centuries. Pugin coated this

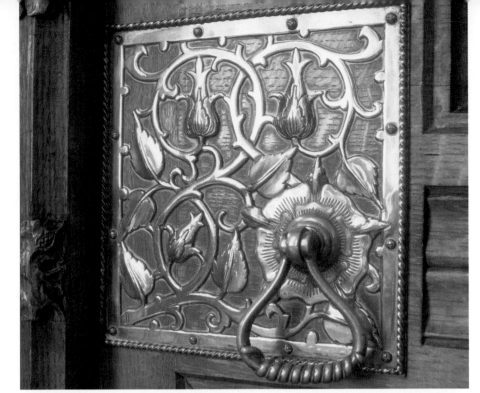

Left The Venetian Drawing Room is decorated with black panelling, painted to look like ebony. This acts as a frame for paintings inspired by Shakespeare's *The Merchant of Venice*. The characters shown here are thought to be Gratiano, friend of Antonio and Bassanio, and Leonardo, servant to Bassanio. **Below left** A heavily studded wooden door opens into the Outer Hall, designed by Edward Pugin. Light streams through the large stained-glass window, which would not look out of place in a church.

Above right Even small decorative details are in keeping with the high-Victorian style of the house. This brass door plate, in the Venetian Drawing Room, is pierced with a sinuous design of twining stems, roses and leaves. **Right** This intricate piece of relief sculpture on the fireplace in the Dining Room shows a bear stealing honey from a hive. The work is incredibly detailed, from the leaves on the trees right down to the hairs on the bear's back and the paw raised to swat away angry bees.

with Gothic embellishments. After his early death in 1875, the interior was fitted out for Beaumont by another Catholic architect, J. F. Bentley, designer of Westminster Cathedral.

The exterior is L-shaped and embattled. Pugin intended a third range, a 'Hall of the Barons', which was never built. He covered most of the exterior in dun-coloured cement, much blackened and scored to look like stone. He added three truly ugly towers and a massive entrance dominating the angle of the L-shape. The doorway is festooned with Gothic ornament derived from the Low Countries, its steps guarded by heraldic beasts holding flags. The left-hand wing has been allowed to acquire modest creeper.

The interior is astonishing. The entrance hall rises past more heraldry to the main hall, or Armoury. This is beamed and painted in over-the-top Gothic motifs. Steps to the right continue up to Bentley's state apartments. The main chamber is the Venetian Drawing Room. Its Gothic chimneypiece is enriched with Stapleton heraldry and its walls are of plaster, stamped and gilded to look like Spanish leather. The black panelling carries scenes from *The Merchant of Venice*. The two rooms beyond are its equal in scale if not in splendour, linked by beautifully crafted Gothic doors. Visitors should arrive mounted and in armour.

Castle **Howard**

★ ★ ★ ★ ☆　Vanbrugh's Baroque palace

5 miles SW of Malton; private house and grounds, open part year

Horace Walpole exclaimed, 'Nobody had informed me that I should at one view see a palace, a town, a fortified city, temples on high places, woods worthy of being each a metropolis of the Druids … and a mausoleum that would tempt one to be buried alive.' The North will never be dull as long as it has Castle Howard. This is not a castle but the true palace of an aristocrat.

The house crowns a spur of the North York Moors. I have seen its limestone glowing in the spring sunshine across fields of daffodils. I have also seen it on a winter dawn, its mane thick with snow, growling defiance at a world that has often told it to lie down and die. Howards built this great house. Howards restored it after a terrible fire, and Howards live there today.

Castle Howard was built by the 3rd Earl of Carlisle, politician and man of culture. He preferred the latter pursuit. It was as a member of the Whig Kit-Cat Club (see Beningbrough Hall, page 37) that he met the young playwright, John Vanbrugh, and told him of his desire for a grand house on his Yorkshire estate. The initial approach appears to have been made in 1699.

Far from any centre of fashion or taste, this would be a castle of delight to draw his friends to what must have seemed an inaccessible wilderness. Carlisle did not like plans previously prepared by William Talman, architect of Chatsworth. Although Vanbrugh had never built a house, he set to work in 1700 with his assistant, Nicholas Hawksmoor. Carlisle resigned all public offices and devoted the rest of his life to the house, which was only half completed on his death in 1738. What many regarded as disaster ensued. The earl's

son-in-law, the Burlingtonian architect, Sir Thomas Robinson, tore up Vanbrugh's Baroque design for completing the west wing and, in the 1750s, began a rectangular west block. He seemed eager to demolish what Vanbrugh had created in what he saw as an old-fashioned style. This new Palladian west wing was not finished until 1811 and the result is a clear imbalance. Even today this so embarrasses the Howards that no picture of the West Wing appears in the guidebook. Worse was to follow. In 1940 a terrible fire broke out in the south-east wing, destroying twenty of the Vanbrugh rooms and the central dome. It took the late Lord Howard the rest of the 20th century to restore the dome. Some rooms remain derelict.

'The North will never be dull as long as it has Castle Howard.'

Castle Howard is regarded, with Blenheim, as a masterpiece of English Baroque. Yet it was a house rooted in the Palladian tradition. Vanbrugh's plan, of a central block with colonnades and wings, was that of a Palladian villa, its rooms along one floor rather than stacked vertically. Yet outside and inside, the house has spacial and decorative movement, planes advancing and receding in Baroque fashion.

The house is entered through Robinson's Georgian wing, with portraits of Howards galore and with two suites of 18th-century bedrooms, each with a magnificent bed. The one in the Castle Howard Bedroom is by John Linnell, sitting well amid the Marco Ricci landscapes on the wall. The bed in Lady Georgiana's Bedroom is extraordinary, like a French chevalier with his legs in the air.

Sir John Vanbrugh
1664-1726

Vanbrugh was a man of many talents. He started out as a soldier but made his name as a playwright, and his success on the stage brought him into contact with some notable men, including the 3rd Earl of Carlisle. Incredibly, he only made the switch to an architectural career when the Earl asked him to design Castle Howard.

Vanbrugh's original design for Castle Howard included two passages that linked different rooms. The passages were effectively corridors, quite an architectural innovation in England in the early 18th century. The Antique Passage, in the West Wing of the house, is lined with artefacts collected mainly by the 4th Earl during his second visit to Italy in 1738–39.

Classical busts brought back from many a Grand Tour line the Antique Passage, like a guard of honour, to the Great Hall. This is the heart of the house, rising 70 feet to the dome. Vanbrugh here plays virtuoso stage designer, with four massive arches rising past balconies to the rotunda and cupola. Spaces recede from these balconies to meet hidden arches beyond. Murals by Pellegrini were repainted after the 1940 fire by a Canadian, Scott Medd. They include *The Four Elements* and *The Fall of Phaeton*, Apollo's son, a play on Carlisle's political fortunes. A fire burns below in a stupendous Baroque fireplace. This is one of England's grandest rooms.

The remaining interiors of Castle Howard are diminuendo. The Garden Hall was restored by the late Lord Howard with money from the filming here of *Brideshead Revisited*. It is in 'the spirit of Vanbrugh', with large capriccios of the house by Felix Kelly. The rooms to the left of the Garden Hall contain an exhibition on the house's restoration.

'This is **not** a **castle but** the **true palace** of an **aristocrat.**'

The 3rd Earl wanted the grounds of Castle Howard to provide a suitable setting for Vanbrugh's masterpiece and much of the parkland and gardens were developed while the house was being built. Contemporary taste called for a rolling naturalistic landscape that would offer views of the great house glimpsed through trees or across water. The South Lake, which was created in the early 1720s, provides visitors to the park with a double image of Castle Howard's palatial façade.

The reception rooms to the right survived the fire and contain the family's art collection. This includes works by Reynolds, Gainsborough and, in the Orleans Room, Canaletto, Rubens, Claude Lorraine and Holbein. The final Museum Room is filled with 19th-century paintings by Watts and Leighton, and by the 9th Earl, artist, Liberal and enthusiast for the later Pre-Raphaelites.

The corner here turns into the Georgian wing. Robinson's Long Gallery was decorated in 1811 and is punctuated by a central dome. Here hang more Howards and Italian landscapes by Pannini. The tour ends with the 18th-century private chapel, still in use. This was boldly redecorated at the end of the 19th century with embroidery by Morris, windows by Burne-Jones and murals to designs by C. E. Kempe. In the lobby outside is a delightful small museum of curiosities, such as a stuffed monkey, an ornamental wheelbarrow, a bleeding bowl and many commemorative trowels and spades.

The grounds at Castle Howard are as celebrated as the house. To the east lies the famous Ray Wood with its unique collection of rare trees and shrubs. Vistas are dotted with Vanbrughian towers, obelisks and pyramids, including his Temple of the Four Winds, and Hawksmoor's Mausoleum, the finest in England and a palace in itself.

Left The Mausoleum was begun long before the 3rd Earl's death and was an important part of his plans for Castle Howard. It was designed by Nicholas Hawksmoor, Vanbrugh's assistant on the main house, and building began in 1729. The work was not finished until the 1740s, after both the Earl and Hawksmoor were dead. Six years after his death, the Earl finally had his wish and was interred in the mausoleum.

Right The Great Hall rises up through the heart of Castle Howard to its magnificent dome. Painted inside the cupola is *The Fall of Phaeton*, originally by the Venetian artist Giovanni Pellegrini and restored by Scott Medd in the 1960s. Pellegrini (and later Medd) was also responsible for *The Four Elements*, which are painted below the dome's gallery in the spaces between the arches. *Fire*, holding a blazing urn, can be seen here in the centre, while *Earth*, bearing an orb, is on the right.

Fire and restoration

On the morning of 9th November 1940 tragedy struck Castle Howard when a fire broke out in the south-east wing. At first it was thought that the flames could be confined to that wing, but then the wind got up and the fire spread into the Great Hall and the centre of the house. The dome and nearly twenty of the rooms were destroyed in the blaze.

In the years immediately after the fire it appeared that Castle Howard might remain empty and neglected, especially since two of the heirs to the property had been killed during World War II. Fortunately, the remaining heir, George Howard, returned from wartime service determined to restore the house to its former glory. Over the years he worked to rebuild Castle Howard, work that his heirs continue today.

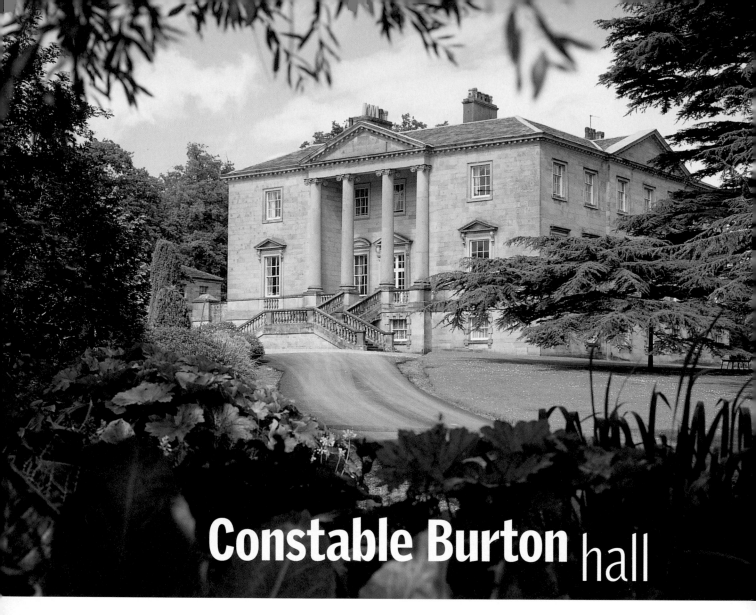

Constable Burton hall

⭐ Palladian house by John Carr of York, set in parkland

3 miles E of Leyburn; private house, gardens open part year

The drive from the road is through open farmland and into dense ornamental woods. Two magnificent cedars part and reveal a villa that might be in the Italian Veneto. A double flight of stairs rises from the forecourt to the entrance, recessed behind four columns and a portico. There is a single, wide bay on either side. This is not a big house and it is almost as pure in its Palladianism as if by Inigo Jones.

Constable Burton – not to be confused with Burton Constable (see page 21) – was designed by Carr of York for Sir Marmaduke Wyvill, *c*1762. It is said that Wyvill went on the Grand Tour leaving strict instructions for Carr to repair his old house, not build a new one. Like many an architect, Carr appears to have 'misunderstood'. He was presumably forgiven and Wyvills occupy the house to this day.

Although the building is not open to visitors, they can perambulate the splendid exterior from the surrounding gardens. Parking is in front of the house and there is no sense of exclusion. The grounds embrace an extensive collection of maple and conifer along terraces flanking the slope down to a river. The finest view of the house is from across the park. It is attended by a magnificent copper beech, standing like a rich uncle, noticeable yet never out of place.

Crathorne hall

At Crathorne, 2 miles S of Yarm; now a hotel

The house cuts a dash on a bluff over the River Leven, south of Middlesbrough. It was one of the last grand houses of the Edwardian era, built for the cotton tycoon Lionel Dugdale, between 1903 and 1906. The architect was the Queen Anne revivalist, Sir Ernest George. There were 115 rooms, including 41 bedrooms, and the Dugdales had a staff of 26 indoor servants.

Dugdale's ambitious wife ensured that her daughter became a countess and her son, Thomas, became the local MP, marrying the elegant Nancy Tennant. On Lionel's death in 1941, Thomas Dugdale turned Crathorne Hall into a centre of political entertainment. His ministerial career ended with the Crichel Down affair in 1954. (He is forever remembered as the last politician to accept personal responsibility for a mistake made by his civil servant.)

After Thomas Dugdale's death in 1977, Crathorne Hall became a hotel. The younger members of the family sent the house off with a huge Edwardian Ball, saying goodbye to the place 'in a blaze of light'.

The entrance façade is Vanbrugh-revival, the porch rusticated and with a segmental roof. Massive neo-Jacobean towers fill the two angles of the courtyard. The garden front is again after Vanbrugh, with a lofty armorial pediment supported by an Ionic colonnade. A wrought-iron balcony adorns the first floor. The whole composition looks confidently over the surrounding landscape as if Dugdales and houses like this were for ever. England in the 1900s had not a care in the world.

The interior is well mannered. The vestibule, with a barrel vault, acts as corridor to the main reception rooms. The central drawing room has Dugdale heraldry over the fireplace and pilastered doorways. The walls have thankfully retained their family portraits, including some by Nancy Dugdale herself. In the dining room is a superb landscape by Miles Birkett Foster.

Duncombe park

★★★ Baroque mansion with post-fire Victorian interiors

At Helmsley, 12 miles E of Thirsk; private house and grounds,
open part year (house by guided tour only)

The landscape of Rievaulx, Helmsley and Duncombe is among the most celebrated in England. Abbey, castle and great house once stood separate, but were brought together in the 18th century by Duncombe money and the collective genius of English architecture.

Sir Charles Duncombe was a Restoration banker, tax collector and reputedly the richest commoner in England. He bought the entire Helmsley estate in 1689, shortly before being committed briefly to the Tower of London for fraud. After his death in 1711, his nephew, Thomas Browne, adopted the Duncombe name and commissioned a grand house in the rolling landscape behind Rievaulx. The builder was William Wakefield but the inspirer, it is thought, was Vanbrugh, then working at Castle Howard. The palatial west front is undeniably Vanbrughian, as is the robust portico on the east front. The west is now the entrance, reached up a flight of steps from the courtyard. The flanking service wings are later, by Sir Charles Barry.

The interior was destroyed by fire in 1879. Thomas Duncombe's descendant, the Earl of Feversham, rebuilt it in 1895, employing William Young, architect of town halls and of country houses that look like town halls. Only the main hall reappeared as it had been. The rest was replaced in the French Empire style. The hall rises the full height of the house, its bare stone walls punctuated by openings and adorned with classical medallions. Two gigantic fireplaces are surmounted by urns in niches. It is strongly reminiscent of the hall at Castle Howard.

The rebuilt saloon was draped in the heaviest of Continental furnishings, thick with palms and aspidistras. The effect, says the admirable guidebook, was to create 'for the humble Earl and Countess of Feversham the agreeable illusion that they were Louis XVI and Marie Antoinette on vacation in Hawaii'. The pillars and oak panels with gilded swags seem more an assembly room in the style of Wren than a saloon.

The room leads into the more intimate withdrawing room. A picture by Andrea Soldi depicts the Georgian, Charles Duncombe, as a boy holding a pheasant. Legend relates that he overheard a village girl singing, 'What e'er may

Above In the main hall female figures and putti recline on top of the arches that punctuate the stone walls. They bear medallions made of plaster that were painted to resemble stone. **Below** This Doric Temple was built at the south end of a great landscaped terrace overlooking Helmsley Castle, the original seat of the Duncombe estate. An Ionic Rotunda lies at the other end of the terrace. The Duncombe Terrace prefigures that built by the second Thomas Duncombe to overlook Rievaulx (see page 86).

come, what e'er may fall,/ I will be mistress of Duncombe Hall.' He fell in love with her on the spot and married her. The ever-lively guidebook suggests the scene would now have to take place in 'some kind of out-of-town shopping precinct'.

The dining room contains flamboyant portraits of Feversham girls in their Victorian prime by Edward Hughes. Hermione, Duchess of Leinster, was considered 'the most beautiful woman in England' by that connoisseur of these matters, Edward VII. Other rooms on show include the library and upstairs bedrooms.

There could have been no better era in which to restore a great house than the late 19th century. Art was confident and craftsmanship meticulous. The teak windows at Duncombe have never needed replacing, despite the house's sixty years as a girls' school after the Great War. The present Lord Feversham has restored the house as his family home.

Fountains abbey

✦ ✦ Surviving ruins of a great monastery

At Studley Royal, 3 miles SW of Ripon;
National Trust, open all year

Which to prefer, Fountains or Rievaulx? I am marginally for Rievaulx, although on a misty autumn day the majestic outline of Fountains Abbey with its defiant tower, erected on the brink of the Dissolution, is hard to beat. Thirteen monks arrived in 1132 from the Benedictine St Mary's, York, switching their loyalty to the new Cistercian order. Their inspirer was Geoffrey of Clairvaux, expert in monastic foundation. He had already begun Rievaulx two years earlier. Despite the wildness of the place, the new community was to extend its domain over a hundred square miles of Yorkshire, prospering here for four centuries.

The ruins of Fountains are among the most complete of any English monastery, largely because of their remoteness. They are now a World Heritage site and owned by the National

Below Adjacent to Fountains Abbey is the Studley Royal Water Garden, a Georgian landscaped garden that makes full use of the ruined abbey's picturesque potential.

'... the **storeroom** is no less impressive, a long double nave of **rib-vaults** in bare stone, **ascetic** in the extreme.'

Trust. Most of the residential ranges can still be discerned either on the ground or in standing walls. Of these, the finest is the ruined dormitory, 300 ft long, with its storeroom beneath. The western prospect of this range, dating from the late 12th century, was to Pevsner 'one of the most impressive experiences of monastic architecture in England … a world of exacting order unmatched in the secular world'.

The building stretched unbroken from the west end of the church to the River Skell. The inside of the storeroom is no less impressive, a long double nave of rib-vaults in bare stone, ascetic in the extreme.

Of the other ranges, only the refectory walls survive, but the adjacent warming room is complete, with its vaulted roof and large fireplace. From here stairs lead up to windows, fireplaces and walls, all paying obedience to the great church next door.

These places are no more than stage-sets of a vanished lifestyle and a vanished supremacy. I did once glimpse how they might have been, in the strongly monastic Himalayan kingdom of Bhutan. The answer is noisy, dirty, introverted and obsessively conservative. But they enjoyed an astonishing longevity and left the most impressive early medieval architecture in England.

FOUNTAINS

Fountains hall

✦✦ A late Smythson mansion in the grounds of Fountains Abbey

At Studley Royal, 3 miles SW of Ripon; National Trust, open all year

To reach Fountains Hall, the Fountains Abbey visitor centre, which might be in a zoo, must first be breached. There follows a walk across the rolling acres of the Abbey estate to Skelldale. Here is a cluster of buildings by a bridge where, behind warm stone walls and yew hedges, lies Fountains Hall, still heartbreakingly empty.

The hall was built in 1611 by Sir Stephen Proctor, son of a lead and coal magnate. Proctor was a fierce Calvinist and hunter-down of recusants. In this role he was created 'Collector of Fines on Penal Statutes', his qualifications

Duke of York, later George VI. The house became a school before being acquired by the local council in 1966. It passed to the National Trust in 1983 but only the hall and ground floor are open to the public at present.

The front to the formal garden is Smythson at his most complex and mature. The garden is entered by a pretty gateway through magnificent yews that accentuate the towers of the house against the green hillside behind. The façade is a series of projecting and receding planes with castellated flanking bays and wide windows.

being of an 'unscrupulous and unsqueamish' temperament. He was hated locally and two attempts were made on his life. He robustly adopted as his motto, 'Finding nothing, I will earn everything'. He built himself a new house in the grounds of Fountains Abbey to designs ascribed to the elderly Robert Smythson. By 1620 Proctor had vanished, whether killed or bankrupted, nobody knows.

The Aislabie family acquired the Fountains Estate in 1767, their main house already being at Studley Royal. Sadly, Fountains Hall was allowed to fall into disuse. It was restored by the Vyner family in the 1930s and was even considered as a Yorkshire seat for the then

The central bay is sensational. As at Hardwick Hall (Derbyshire), everything is an expanse of glass, including the bow window lighting the Great Chamber. Yet there is something eccentric about this house. The two sides do not quite balance, as if a wayward local mason were determined to medievalize Smythson's plan.

The frontispiece is crowded with Renaissance statuary and heraldry. The door is up hidden steps, sideways on to the front, and gives into a screens passage and asymmetrical Great Hall. The rooms inside are empty, except for display boards. Upstairs, the Great Chamber contains a superb ceiling and Renaissance overmantel depicting the Judgment of Solomon.

Hazlewood castle

'It is supremely stylish.'

★★ Restored medieval castle with interiors by John Carr of York

3 miles SW of Tadcaster; now a hotel

If Hazlewood is the future for many English houses, it will not be dull. Until 1996 the castle was run as a Carmelite monastic retreat, and it is now a luxury hotel, teamed with a cookery school and conference centre. The reception boasts 'a distinctly different lifestyle experience'. My guide broke off to carry a guest's case upstairs.

This was the ancestral home of the Vavasour family, who survived the Wars of the Roses, recusancy, Popish plotting and the Civil War, but could not survive 20th-century financial ineptitude. The old house was sold in 1908. A succession of later owners were sympathetic to its architecture and, luckily, to its religion, with the house passing to the Carmelite Order in 1967. The house remains in excellent condition.

The main façade is a Georgian refacing of a medieval Great Hall, probably attached to a pele tower at the rear. Today, the present Hall is classical, reached by a wide flight of steps and Doric doorway. It is supremely stylish. The conversion was reputedly by Carr of York. There are green walls flanked with columns on all four sides, rising to coved arches beneath a bold Jacobean ceiling. In each arch is a roundel displaying the Vavasour arms. The windows are big and flood the room with light. A fragment of medieval wall survives in one bay.

Behind this Hall is the present hotel entrance, known as the Flemish Hall. This was created in the 1960s and lined with 17th-century Flemish panelling from a Carmelite church in Ghent. The panels depict the lives of saints and are of high quality. In the centre of the wall facing the entrance is the famous Jezebel fireplace brought from Heath Old Hall when it was demolished in 1961. Lucky Hazlewood.

Next door is a small rotunda, again attributed to Carr of York, as are the dining room and staircase. Behind the rotunda is a library in the base of the old pele, with an amusing fake door. Of the smaller reception rooms, the finest is the Victoria Room with 'metallic' wallpaper and a curious hooded fireplace, again installed in the 1960s. The castle was a maternity hospital during the war and this was the delivery ward. Many local women were called Hazel in its honour.

The adjacent 13th-century chapel was redecorated in the Carr style in about 1770 and is still in use for Catholic worship.

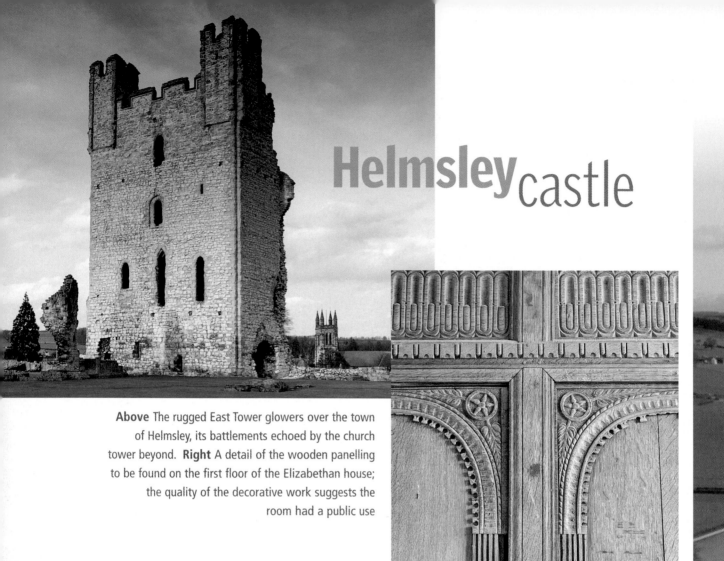

Helmsley castle

Above The rugged East Tower glowers over the town of Helmsley, its battlements echoed by the church tower beyond. **Right** A detail of the wooden panelling to be found on the first floor of the Elizabethan house; the quality of the decorative work suggests the room had a public use

☆ Medieval castle with remains of an Elizabethan mansion

At Helmsley, 12 miles E of Thirsk; English Heritage, open all year

The castle was begun by the Norman magnate, Walter Espec, Lord of Helmsley, to guard the River Rye. Its massive bastions gaze across the acres of Duncombe Park towards the great house and the terraces above Rievaulx. The keep can be seen for miles around. Espec is said to have built the first fortification at the same time as he invited the Cistercians to found Rievaulx Abbey in 1132. The earliest buildings are attributed to the de Roos family, from the end of the 12th century. The family held the castle until 1508.

An impressive double ditch surrounds the site, forming a deep slope on which children are still allowed to play (pending the arrival of the health-and-safety spoilsports). The curtain wall is entered by a strong barbican, parts of which have been allowed to retain their creeper. Inside the bailey is the D-shaped keep, neatly sliced in half by the Roundheads after a prolonged siege in 1644. It retains a vaulted ground floor and relics of upper chambers are visible in the wall.

More remarkable is the survival of a late Elizabethan house on the opposite side of the bailey. This appears to be the solar tower of a ruined Great Hall. It has four storeys and contains Tudor windows and fireplaces. Next to it is a more ordinary Elizabethan house. This has a ground floor chamber with timbered partitions. Upstairs are two rooms with panelling and decorative plasterwork. This was the distant predecessor of Duncombe Park (see page 52).

Below From the air, viewed here from the south, Helmsley's history is laid out. The oldest parts of the castle, dating from the early 12th century, are the massive earthworks that surround the site. The ruined East Tower and the remains of a curtain wall that runs around the inner bailey were built at the very end of the same century. The South Barbican was added in the middle of the 13th century to bolster the castle's defences. To the west lie the remains of a 14th-century tower and hall, and the 16th-century Elizabethan mansion.

Hovingham hall

Above A game of cricket is played out on the lawn at Hovingham, possibly the oldest private cricket ground in England. **Above left** The gateway to the Riding School, at the heart of Hovingham Hall. **Left** Attention to detail, as on these finely worked classical columns and capitals, characterizes the decoration inside the hall.

 Palladian stables with house attached

At Hovingham, 8 miles W of Malton; private house and grounds, open part year

If Caligula could make his horse a consul, the Worsleys could make their stables a home. Hovingham is as odd as any house in England. It sits, French style, in the centre of its village rather than at a distance outside it. More eccentric, its entrance is (or was) through a riding school leading to a dismounting hall. Horses were to be stabled on either side, where normally would have been the 'rustic' family rooms beneath the state rooms above. Family and guests were to be housed in wings.

The creator of the house was Thomas Worsley, amateur architect and professional horseman. He had studied these vocations in Switzerland and, having inherited from his father in 1750, determined to put both to good use at Hovingham. Although he held the sinecure of Surveyor-General at the Office of Works from 1760, and thus had access to London craftsmen, he drew up his own plans for his new house.

His model was Palladio's proposed 'reconstruction' of a Roman house, with courtyards, atrium and rectangular vestibules. He built the riding school and central stable block but had added only one residential wing when building ceased. He then found stables were not ideal so near a house – they smelled – and moved them back into the courtyard. The result was a hopeless mess.

60

The dismounting hall was an important feature of the original design for Hovingham. The idea was that riders would not need to get down from their mounts until they were inside. Stabling for the horses was arranged on either side. The hall was a vaulted, airy space, based upon a classic Roman loggia. Today this entrance is known as the Samson Hall and is decorated with classical statues, arranged on plinths.

Today, Worsley's obsession with horses – he also ran a stud farm – is everywhere on display. The disused Riding School remains the pride of the place in the middle of the composition. Each end has a Tuscan screen and loggia, from one of which guests could watch horses performing without standing in a muddy courtyard. Beyond would normally have been the house entrance and hall, but instead there is the paved Samson Hall, supposedly for dismounting, modelled on a Roman loggia with groin vaults. On either side are the intended horse boxes. These are now vestibules, one with a fine array of tapestries.

The rooms above the Samson Hall include reception rooms and a ballroom. The ballroom has grisaille murals by Sebastiano Ricci and Cipriani. Next door is a pretty Ionic Room, its walls crowded with pictures hung in the Georgian manner. Hovingham's collection includes works by van Dyck, Poussin and Boucher, which might sink without trace in a large museum yet are a delight to find scattered round a family house.

These rooms are necessarily removed from the family quarters, always in the side wing. The former state bedroom has become the dining room, hung with Worsleys from the 18th to the 20th centuries. The fireplaces and capitals are of excellent workmanship, allegedly from Worsley's London craftsmen.

On the lawn outside is one of the oldest family cricket pitches in England. The view up the valley embraces the remains of a classical landscape with a fine Palladian bridge.

Kiplin hall

✩ ✩ A Jacobean mansion with 19th-century alterations

At Kiplin, 5 miles E of Catterick; private house, open part year

The redoubtable Bridget Talbot died in 1971. A socialist, Red Cross volunteer and fierce defender of Kiplin, she set up a charitable trust to preserve the old house after her death. With insufficient endowment, this could be achieved only by the drastic measure of digging up its park as a gravel quarry. Today, the quarry has gone, replaced by a graceful lake, with a folly on an island and fishermen on the bank. The National Trust refused the house as too 'Victorian' and the Kiplin Hall Trust, the gravel exhausted, struggles on as best it can.

George Calvert, 1st Lord Baltimore, and founder of Maryland in America, built Kiplin between 1622 and 1625. It is nearly a square, with projecting towers and cupolas not on each corner but in the middle of each side. This verticality happily left the main chambers filled with light from two sides, and the central space free of staircases. The façades are of redbrick with diaper patterning, the entrance flanked by handsome paired columns. The symmetry of the 'box' is spoilt only by a large library of 1818 built to one side.

The interiors and much of the exterior brickwork are Victorian. A Kiplin heiress married John Carpenter, the 4th Earl Tyrconnel, in 1817. Having no heir, she fastened on a young naval cousin, a member of the Catholic Talbot family, as inheritor of the estate. Her will required him both to become a Protestant and to marry one, a pledge subject to a seven-yearly investigation by a team of Anglican clergymen. He should also change his name from Talbot to Carpenter. All this he did. He rose to the rank of admiral and his memorabilia fill some of the rooms. Eden Nesfield was brought in to modernize the house and build the fine stables.

In the library is a school of van Dyck of Charles II. Paintings in the dining room are by G. F. Watts and Angelica Kauffmann. The staircase inserted in the 18th century leads to a pleasant series of domestic rooms upstairs, including a sitting room filled with watercolours by another Talbot relative, Lady Waterford. A Long Gallery looks out over the restored park. Many of the rooms are still in the process of restoration and refurnishing.

Kirkleatham: Turner's hospital

✦ Georgian almshouses with Baroque chapel

At Kirkleatham, 2 miles S of Redcar;
private retirement home, restricted opening

Sir William Turner was the Lord Mayor of
London charged with rebuilding the City
after the Great Fire. He was also a Yorkshireman.
He died in 1692 and his family's house has been
demolished. Other buildings survive. The church
and Turner mausoleum, by James Gibbs, defied
the wreckers. The Free School, erected in 1708
after Turner's death, is a magnificent two-storey
structure with a giant pedimented central door.
And there are the almshouses.

Although a man of standing in London,
Turner acknowledged his duties to his home
village. The hospital he founded in 1676 was

Right This statue of an elderly lady would have welcomed
the female residents of Sir William Turner's almshouses
in the days when the accommodation was segregated,
with men and women living in separate wings.
The building was a 'hospital' in the archaic sense of the
word; it offered hospitality, and was a refuge for those
local inhabitants too old to look after themselves.

mostly rebuilt by his descendant, Cholmley Turner, in 1742. The present almshouses are among the finest of the period in England. They do not display the usual cottage quadrangle but comprise three ranges around an open courtyard. Pride of place goes to the tower above the chapel, with schoolrooms arranged to its left and right. The courtyard is flanked by two wings, for twelve men and twelve women each, of brick with stone dressings. Each culminates in a substantial house for the master and mistress respectively. Stone statues of an old man and an old woman adorn these houses, possibly carved by Scheemakers. The courtyard is open to the road, with ornamental railings and gates.

The chapel is a Baroque gem. The central tower rises over the porch. Inside is a square interior with Ionic columns worthy of a Wren church in the City of London. At the west end, a gallery rises up steps to a magnificent doorway, above which presides a bust in honour of Cholmley Turner, a dramatic touch. The carvings are 'after Gibbons' and the doors Rococo. Nothing was too good for the people of Kirkleatham in those days.

'The **chapel** is a **Baroque** gem.'

Left Facing his female counterpart across the courtyard, this statue of an old man stood guardian to the male quarters. The almshouses have been in continuous use since they were built and still operate as a retirement home. And for two-and-a-half centuries, up until the middle of World War II, Turner's Hospital also offered free schooling and accommodation for twenty children, ten girls and ten boys who were trained, respectively, for domestic and naval service.

Knaresborough: House in the rock

Above One of Britain's most unusual dwellings, the House in the Rock perches high above the River Nidd, built into the cliff that plunges into the river gorge. **Right** Nearby is the Shrine of Our Lady of the Crag, thought to be the third oldest wayside shrine in Britain. It was built, it is claimed, by a local man, John the Mason, who cut it out of the cliffs where his son survived a rockfall.

 Curious Georgian home set into a cliff face

At Knaresborough, 5 miles NE of Harrogate; private house, restricted opening

In 1774 a linen weaver called Thomas Hill built himself a house in a cleft in the rock overlooking Knaresborough gorge and the River Nidd. Here he lived with his wife and six children, in four rooms stacked on top of each other. His descendants owned the house until 1916, castellating it and renaming it Fort Montague. It was bequeathed to Ampleforth Abbey, owner of the adjacent chapel, and opened as a curiosity and tea-room. The house was sold in 2000 and has now been painstakingly restored and modernised.

The house's location is superb, with a picturesque drama more common to the river gorges of France than England. Next door is the Shrine of Our Lady of the Crag. This tiny chapel was hewn from the rock in 1409 as a thank offering for a local boy who was saved from death in a rockfall by an apparition of the Virgin Mary. It has been a place of pilgrimage, on and off, ever since.

Markenfield hall

★★★ An early 14th-century moated farmstead

3 miles SW of Ripon; private house and grounds, open part year

The small settlement sits alone in fields south of Ripon, looking much as it did when built in the 14th century. While most such fortified farms were extensively altered in the 16th century and later, Markenfield is mostly medieval. It has been beautifully restored and its chapel reconsecrated. From the roof of the solar is an uninterrupted rural view.

The builder was John of Markenfield, Chancellor to the hapless Edward II. The house needed to be fortified to protect him from his (or the King's) local enemies, licence being duly granted in 1310. The family was devoutly Catholic and were leaders of the anti-Protestant Rising of the North from Ripon. They lost the house in the process. In the 17th century, Markenfield passed to the Grantleys of nearby Grantley Hall, who occupy it to this day in the name of Curteis.

The house is like an apparition across the fields. Two farm buildings flank a track over a wide moat to an imposing stone wall. Here a two-storey Tudor gatehouse guards the

entrance to the inner courtyard. The old house is in the right-hand corner, at an angle to the Great Hall directly ahead. This hall is on the first floor, with kitchens and storage underneath. The ghost of an old outside doorway can be seen in its wall. Its windows have 14th-century tracery.

The Great Hall interior has lost most of its medieval features. The roof is 18th century and the staircase from the undercroft below is Victorian. The adjacent restored chapel has one of the loveliest small piscinas that I have seen in any church. It is proudly multi-denominational, a recent service being attended by one Catholic, one Anglican and one Methodist. Bedrooms and sitting rooms have been fitted into the chapel tower and the medieval chambers below. Old rib-vaults have been restored. Furniture is being assembled. Markenfield is a rare treasure in the hands of dedicated custodians.

Above Among the features of the chapel at Markenfield is a rare double piscina, set in a niche in the wall. One basin was for washing the chalice after mass, the other was for washing the priest's hands; church law forbade the use of the same water for both functions, hence the double basin. The coat of arms on the front of the piscina is that of John de Markenfield, who built the house in 1310. The inclusion of the three coins was intended as a reference to Markenfield's role as Chancellor of the Exchequer.

'Here a **Juliet** might **listen to** her **Romeo singing** in the lane below. It is a **magical** spot.'

Marmion tower

 Medieval tower with oriel window

At West Tanfield, 6 miles NW of Ripon; English Heritage, open all year

The tower lies sandwiched down a lane between a wild garden running down to the River Ure and St Nicholas Church in West Tanfield. The church was built curiously close to the walls of the old castle, although it may have been the other way round. A door in the church is dated *c*1200. Either way, the setting is picturesque.

The building was erected as a gateway to the castle in the late 14th century and is clearly decorative rather than defensive. Now accessible and in the care of English Heritage, it is of three storeys. There is a fine fireplace on the ground floor. Stairs built into the corner masonry lead to the roof and look-out. A projecting latrine faces the river while a pretty oriel window floods light into the first floor chamber. Here a Juliet might listen to her Romeo singing in the lane below. It is a magical spot.

Middleham castle

★ Extensive ruins of Richard III's northern fortress

At Middleham, 2 miles S of Leyburn; English Heritage, open all year

The small town of Middleham guards the approach to Coverdale. While racehorses stalk through the main street on their way to the gallops, the great fortress in which Richard III spent his youth still broods over its south flank. Although a ruin, it is a most evocative medieval structure. To stand on the platform of Middleham keep and look into its cavernous Great Hall is to gaze into a dark corner of history.

The castle was built by Alan, post-Conquest Lord of Richmond, to assert his authority over the Dales. The present keep was constructed a century later in the 1170s, and is among the most massive of its period. A suite of chambers is divided between Great Hall and Great Chamber, with associated kitchens and ante-rooms.

Another century later, the castle passed to the Nevills, who built an outer curtain wall and developed the space inside it. The castle was Richard III's northern headquarters and was duly seized by Henry VII after Bosworth. It never recovered its former glory.

Although unroofed, Middleham has a mighty presence, its silhouette largely intact. The gatehouse leads into the outer courtyard, surrounded by the remains of the late medieval settlement. In the centre rises the vast keep, with stairs leading down to kitchens and up to a view of the Great Hall. From the roof is a superb view over the castle to Wensleydale. The hoofbeats of history still echo round these walls.

Above Within the castle is what remains of a horse pit. This was an early means of harnessing horsepower, in this case to help with grinding corn. A horse would have walked in a circle, pushing or pulling a mechanism that ran around the circular trough in the stone floor. The pit suggests that corn was ground on a large scale here and that the castle must have been home to many people.

'The façade of the house is a delight.'

☆ Dutch-gabled house with florid staircase

At Moulton, 2 miles SE of Scotch Corner; National Trust, open part year

Two houses loom over the little village of Moulton. Both were built in the 1660s, both in an archaic Jacobean style. The private manor is the more conservative, U-plan with gabled wings and small pediments over the windows. Moulton Hall beyond, owned by the National Trust, is the more remarkable. Three flowing Dutch gables peer above a high yew hedge, odd features to find in the Yorkshire countryside. The gables are similar to those applied to Kew Palace in the 1630s. Perhaps these took their cue from those at Norton Conyers (see page 78).

The façade of the house is a delight. The first-floor windows have alternately triangular and segmental hoods. The round windows are off-centre to the gables, as if the mason were unsure of his instructions.

The chief feature of the interior is the staircase, a remarkable construction of 'yeoman's Baroque' built to the rear of the house. It rises in eight flights to fill the entire three storeys of the building. There are finials and pendants in the style of the mid-17th century, the panels a complex work of carving, rich in acanthus leaves. One of the lower panels has the coat of arms of the Peake family, curiously framed by a monstrous open mouth, with nostrils and eyes above it and the lower lips closed by a rope. The symbolism of these torments is obscure.

Moulton hall

Right Although decorated in a style that today might well be called 'monastic minimalism', Cell Eight would have been a fairly comfortable home. The furniture and furnishings were plain and unadorned but any monk who lived there would have a bed to lie on, a table to sit at and curtains to keep out the chill at night.

Mount Grace priory cell eight

★ A monk's cell in a Carthusian monastery

At Staddlebridge, 7 miles NE of Northallerton; English Heritage, open all year

The Carthusians first came to England in 1178, invited by Henry II in penance for the death of Becket, but they expanded rapidly after the Black Death in 1348. The London Charterhouse was founded in 1371 and Mount Grace on the isolated slopes of the Cleveland Hills in 1398.

Dissolved at the Reformation and ruined, the site would be nothing but rubble were it not for the rebuilding of the guests' quarters as a mansion in the 17th century. This was extended and a single cell of the old monastic quarters was restored in 1901. The cell dated from the early years of the 16th century, just before the Dissolution of the monasteries.

The Carthusians were unlike other monks. A closed and solitary order, they lived, worked, prayed and slept in isolation in little cottages round a big central courtyard. This offered security and access for servants. Monks saw each other only for church services. Lay workers brought them food, leaving it in L-shaped cupboards so each could not see the other. This method was also used to collect the product of their labours, for monks spent most of their time earning their keep. This might be copying, book-making, weaving and tailoring. Each monk worked completely alone and the design of the cells prevented any communication.

The two-storey cell is remarkable for its self-sufficiency and comfort. At the rear is a small garden for the growing of herbs and vegetables, as well as a privy with running water. On the ground floor are the living room with fireplace, bedroom and a charming private cloister. Above is the workroom, equipped with a weaving loom. Appropriate furniture has been recreated, herbs grow in the rear garden.

The place is peaceful and moving. I can see why monastic life is enjoying something of a revival. The adjacent 17th-century mansion is now in part a museum.

Newburgh priory

☆ ☆ ☆ Tudor and Jacobean mansion
with Georgian additions

At Coxwold, 7 miles SW of Helmsley;
private house and grounds, open part year

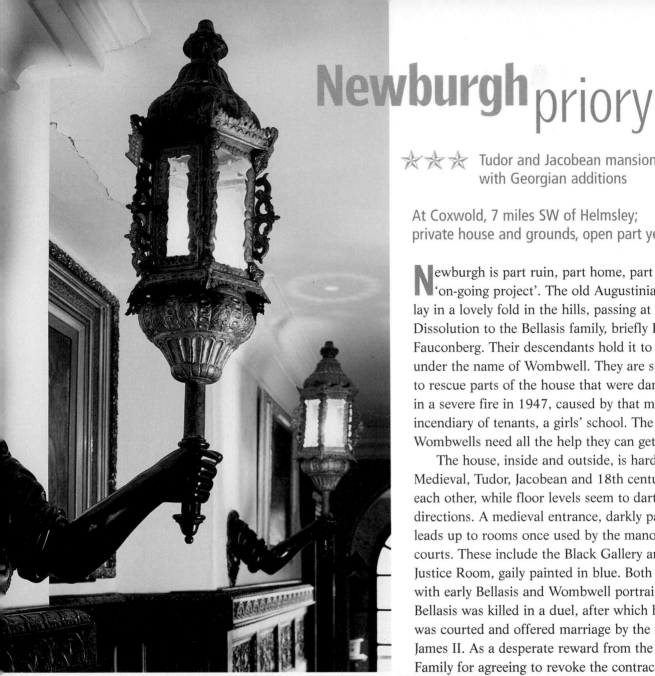

Newburgh is part ruin, part home, part
'on-going project'. The old Augustinian priory
lay in a lovely fold in the hills, passing at the
Dissolution to the Bellasis family, briefly Earls of
Fauconberg. Their descendants hold it to this day
under the name of Wombwell. They are struggling
to rescue parts of the house that were damaged
in a severe fire in 1947, caused by that most
incendiary of tenants, a girls' school. The
Wombwells need all the help they can get.

The house, inside and outside, is hard to read.
Medieval, Tudor, Jacobean and 18th century jostle
each other, while floor levels seem to dart in all
directions. A medieval entrance, darkly panelled,
leads up to rooms once used by the manorial
courts. These include the Black Gallery and the
Justice Room, gaily painted in blue. Both are hung
with early Bellasis and Wombwell portraits. One
Bellasis was killed in a duel, after which his wife
was courted and offered marriage by the future
James II. As a desperate reward from the Royal
Family for agreeing to revoke the contract, she
was given a barony in her own right.

The house is full of surprises. A cosy study
is furnished in memory of the 4th Wombwell
baronet, who survived the Charge of the Light
Brigade despite having had two horses killed
under him. Up a warren of stairs, past doors and

Above Massive lanterns, like those that would have lit the way
for a Venetian gondolier, illuminate Newburgh Priory.
Below The different styles in the house are clearly visible. At the
centre, with the red roof, is the original priory, with Jacobean
windows and a tower to the right. A bow-fronted Tudor addition
is on the far right, while left of the priory is a Georgian wing.

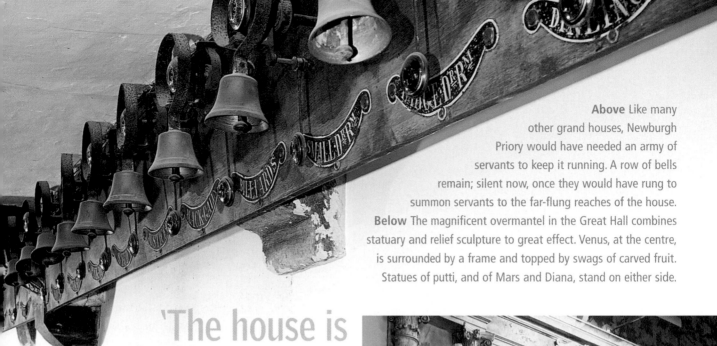

Above Like many other grand houses, Newburgh Priory would have needed an army of servants to keep it running. A row of bells remain; silent now, once they would have rung to summon servants to the far-flung reaches of the house.
Below The magnificent overmantel in the Great Hall combines statuary and relief sculpture to great effect. Venus, at the centre, is surrounded by a frame and topped by swags of carved fruit. Statues of putti, and of Mars and Diana, stand on either side.

'The house is full of surprises.'

thick walls is 'Cromwell's Tomb', by tradition never to be opened. His body was reputedly brought here, possibly minus his head, by his third daughter Mary, Lady Fauconberg. Even a visiting Prince of Wales, later Edward VII, could not induce an estate worker to open it.

Large gondola lanterns lend an exotic touch to the main staircase which contains a display of portraits and china. The passage beneath is panelled by estate carpenters with delightful depictions of local landscapes. The Great Hall, now the dining room, has portraits of Mary Cromwell and Lord Fauconberg gazing down on it.

The prize of this room, perhaps of the house, is a Renaissance overmantel depicting Mars and Diana on pedestals between pillars. They look at each other across a semi-recumbent Venus, evincing a *Country Life* eulogy that there was 'nothing comparable with this in contemporary English sculpture'. The carver is believed to be Nicholas Stone.

Unfortunately, the grand rooms added to the side of the old house in the 1760s were gutted by the fire in 1947. There has never been the money to restore them. They present a tragic spectacle of missing floors, blackened beams and fluted pilasters floating in space.

Beneath them survives an indication of their lost glory: the Small Drawing Room has a superb plasterwork ceiling by Joseph Cortese and paintings of a stag hunt by the great animal painter, Frans Snyders. The Large Drawing Room, also with Cortese work, has two magnificent Rococo mirrors. Everywhere are family portraits. Everywhere are ghosts. Much of Newburgh's charm lies in its incompleteness.

Newby hall

★★★★ William-and-Mary house refashioned by John Carr and Robert Adam

3 miles SE of Ripon; private house and gardens, open part year

If Castle Howard is the crown of the North, Newby is a jewel. The estate lies at the foot of the Dales on the banks of the River Ure. The house was completed for Sir Edward Blackett in 1693, redbrick, stone-quoined and with projecting corner pavilions. It was sold in 1748 to William Weddell, a wealthy dilettante. He transformed it in the 1760s with the help of John Carr and then of Robert Adam. This is Adam at his most light-hearted and enjoyable, an architectural cabinet in which to display Newby's treasures.

In the Regency era, the house passed to Weddell's cousin, Thomas Robinson, Lord Grantham and later Earl de Grey. No sooner did he consider alterations to Newby than he inherited Wrest Park (Bedfordshire) and turned his attention there, which was as well for

'This is **Adam** at his most **light-hearted** and **enjoyable**'

Newby. The house passed eventually to relatives of the Marquesses of Northampton, the Comptons, by whom it is owned to this day. This family continuity is the strength of the house. One elderly attendant told me she had been at her post for fifty years, having 'lived' at Newby for almost ninety.

The blue entrance hall is an Adam feast of Roman motifs, in white on sky-blue with a patterned stone floor. This is an introduction to the bold colour schemes introduced by the present Mrs Compton throughout the house. The hall is furnished with tables by Chippendale and an organ case by 'Athenian' Stuart. The boldly decorated Red Passage leads to the drawing room, a perfect late-Georgian chamber flooded with light from the garden. Here hangs a superb Thomas Lawrence of Lady Theodosia Vyner. The yellow dining room is a variation on a theme of Chippendale, with his tables, side-tables and chairs beneath family portraits by Mytens and van Loo.

Stairs lead upstairs to the eccentric Victorian Wing past the 'Chamber Pot' Room, an art form giving full licence to the potter's sense of humour. This wing is a complete contrast to

Above The magnificence of Newby Hall owes much to the work of Robert Adam. Although he was an architect, Adam's earliest successes were in transforming the interiors of older houses. He had already begun work at Harewood House (see page 164) and had several other commissions under his belt before he took on the transformation of Newby in 1767. Part of Adam's genius lay in adapting classical motifs to appeal to contemporary tastes and using them in decorative schemes where they could be rendered in materials as diverse as plaster, stone or metal.

the rest of the house, a dark masculine retreat for those who found Adam and Chippendale too effete. It is a world of guns, racing trophies, hunting bags and dark, smoky recesses. The raised alcove in the billiards room might be an opium den. Here too is a shrine to Mary Vyner's son, killed in 1870 by Greek brigands when his demanded ransom failed to arrive in time. The money was instead devoted to building Burges's magnificent memorial church in the park, surrounded by weeping beeches.

The Motto Bedroom is decorated with French sayings on walls, doors, bath, even water jug. The bedroom sequence includes a Print Bathroom and bedroom, and a Circular Room with ceiling panels from Herculaneum, copied by Weddell's wife. The landing has serene Adam pier-glasses and elongated Ionic pillars and arches. Nothing at Newby is overstated, everything exquisite.

The acanthus-decorated stairs lead down to the Tapestry Room, designed by Adam around a set of Rococo tapestries from the Gobelins factory in France. The contrast between the geometric ceiling and the floral abundance of the tapestries adds to the glory of this room. Adam's work is a frame for tapestries which are themselves frames for their central roundels of the Loves of the Gods. The whole world is a frame. Even the backs of the Chippendale chairs are frames for tapestry flowers.

The library is by Adam, assisted by Angelica Kauffmann and Antonio Zucchi for the paintings and the younger Joseph Rose for the stucco. The room has apses at each end, with Corinthian screens and ceiling roundels. It is more successful than Adam's library at Kenwood House for being clearly true to its purpose. A tweed jacket hangs on a chair. There is wastepaper in the basket and books on the table.

Weddell's Grand Tour statue gallery fills one of the 18th-century wings. Again by Adam, it is a series of immaculate Roman chambers. Plasterwork fills each niche. Statues are not scattered everywhere but correspond with the architecture. Nothing looks cold. The table tops have scagliola flowers and birds. The family in 2002 sold the most important of the statues to pay for the upkeep of the house.

The gardens at Newby are a sequence of interlocking rectangles. Designed by successive generations of Comptons, they are outlined in varieties of evergreen, spreading on either side of an axis from the house to the river.

Below The sublime tapestries in Newby's Tapestry Room create the romantic atmosphere so essential to Rococo style. They were woven in the 1760s by Jacques Neilson at the Gobelins factory, after designs by the Rococo artist, Francois Boucher. Thomas Chippendale was commissioned to provide chairs and sofas to fit the tapestry covers, also made at Gobelins. They are believed to be the only pieces of furniture by Chippendale to still retain their original upholstery.

Norton Conyers

★ ★ ★ Delightfully antiquated 17th-century house

4 miles N of Ripon; private house and garden, open part year

Below An enormous painting hangs in the Hall. It is acknowledged as the masterpiece of Leicestershire artist, John Ferneley (1782–1860). The infamous 7th Baronet, Sir Bellingham Graham, is among the 33 huntsmen portrayed. Each portrait in the painting, whether human, equine or canine, was said to be a remarkable likeness.

'The Hall ... is a study in faded

Right Royalist Sir Richard Graham, whose horse was said to have left this hoofprint on the landing at Norton Conyers, was on the losing side at the battle of Marston Moor on 2nd July, 1644. The King's armies were defeated by the Parliamentarians in what was to be the first decisive engagement of the English Civil War.

There have been Grahams at Norton Conyers since the 17th century, but they seem to cling on by their fingertips. The family has yet to recover from a Victorian 7th Baronet and his fondness for 'fast women and slow horses'. The present Lady Graham calls him 'Number Seven' and blames him for every ill to have afflicted the house. Few places in this book seem so delightfully faded. Norton is a true period piece. Here we are more likely to be garrotted by a cobweb than fleeced by a corporate hostess.

The character of Norton Conyers lies chiefly in its hinterland, in dusty back kitchens and corridors, in the lack of heating and the paucity of plumbing, and in romantic attics, many of them not open to normal public view. The attics run the length of the roof space and deserve a tour in their own right. They are packed with the detritus of centuries, prints stacked against rafters, pictures without number, steamer trunks with exotic labels, shelves of dusty books, boxes, cases, chests, cabinets …

One gable room supposedly incarcerated the Mad Woman of the family, of whom Charlotte Brontë heard tell when she visited Norton Conyers in 1839 as a governess. The house is thus assumed to be the basis for Rochester's Thornfield Hall in *Jane Eyre*, and the Mad Woman to be Mrs Rochester. The gable room still has a rocking chair and hip-bath.

The house is outwardly early 17th century, with render covering old brickwork. The core is earlier, a 16th-century hall house, traces of which can be seen at the rear. The exterior is dominated by four large Dutch gables, topping all three main façades, behind which run the celebrated attics. The classical doorway in the middle of the west façade leads into one side of the old Great Hall, which clearly would not have been the original arrangement.

The Hall, like most of the house, is a study in faded browns and yellows. Grahams of all ages and reputations gaze down from the walls. Above the old refectory table (with marks for shove ha'penny) is a huge painting of the Quorn Hunt by John Ferneley. It was won by the then baronet by lot between those depicted. Opposite is Sir Richard Graham, who fought for the King at Marston Moor and whose horse returned home with him wounded in the saddle. The horse is said to have galloped into the Hall and then tried to carry Sir Richard upstairs to bed, its scorched hoofprint still visible on one of the landings. This staircase was built onto the back of the Hall, presumably in the early 17th century.

The adjacent parlour is now a sitting room and library. In one of these rooms the 4th Baronet died horribly in 1755. He was supposedly poisoned by a cup of tea prepared for his mistress/housekeeper by disgruntled kitchen staff, which he drank by mistake. The upstairs rooms are used to display family costumes.

The Georgian dining room contains family portraits by Romney and Batoni. The plasterwork is liberally covered in wings, the family's crest awarded to an early Graham for his speed in carrying royal dispatches home from Spain. The stables and gardens at Norton Conyers continue in the style of the house, atmospheric and down at heel. In the walled garden is an astonishing eruption of peonies.

rowns and yellows.'

Nunnington hall

Above The Oak Hall is lined with oak and pine panelling that would have been put up during Lord Preston's remodelling of Nunnington in the late 17th century. Originally, the woodwork would have been painted, but this was stripped away during renovations in the 1920s.

★ ★ ★ Mainly Jacobean house with French-inspired façade

At Nunnington, 4 miles SE of Helmsley; National Trust, open part year

Nunnington was briefly the home of Dr Robert Huicke, celebrated as the bold doctor who had to tell Elizabeth I that she would never have children. He became the patron saint of bad news.

Nunnington is utterly tranquil, set at the foot of an incline on the banks of the River Rye, here little more than a stream. The place seems lost between the Vale of York and Pickering. It was never grand enough for its titular owners to occupy and was usually rented. The owners were Grahams, Viscounts Preston, until the 19th century and then a Liverpool family, the Rutsons, who did not use it until the 1920s. It passed to the National Trust in the 1950s. The last Rutson heiress married a big game hunter named Fife, whose trophies adorn the Stone Hall. Fifes still live on the estate. The attic is used for a collection of miniature objects, firmly described as 'not dolls' houses'.

The history of Nunnington is in its walls. The earliest house is visible to the side, where a jumble of chimneys and gables rises above the entrance to the old Stone Hall. Quite different is the south front facing the garden. It was added by Lord Preston in the 1680s, probably on his return from a brief stay as Charles II's ambassador to France and before his imprisonment as confidant of James II. Work on Nunnington appears to have ceased in 1688.

No one returned from the Paris of Louis XIV untouched by building mania. While the Duke of Montagu sought a Versailles at Boughton (Northamptonshire), the French influence at Nunnington

Below Thought to be built on the site of an earlier 16th-century Great Hall, the Stone Hall once did service as a kitchen, probably after the 17th-century additions to the house. Now it is the first room visited on a tour of Nunnington Hall. Fine pieces of simple wood furniture are arranged around the room and big-game trophies line the walls.

Above The Panelled Bedroom is clad in wood panels dating mostly from the 1630s, although the work around the fireplace is probably later. There is a small oratory off this bedroom and both chambers can claim hauntings by a ghostly presence. Below A minute carpenter's shop, complete with Lilliputian tools, is part of the collection of miniature rooms at Nunnington.

was confined to a pretty ironwork balcony over the front door and the rusticated walls and gate piers. Conservative England remained in the wide gabled wings and heavy chimneys.

The interiors retain their 17th-century character. The Stone Hall was converted into a kitchen when the new hall was added on the south side. The dining room begins the Preston range, with original panelling painted turquoise. On the walls are mezzotints of Reynolds portraits. The 'new' Oak Hall fills the centre of the range, its panelling stripped in the 1920s. A French chimneypiece is another ghost of Preston's Paris years. A screen of three arches leads to a wide staircase with shallow treads, hung with French tapestries.

The upstairs drawing room was once Preston's Great Chamber, since divided into two. The rest of this floor is for wandering. Nunnington's charm lies in spotting the joins between the periods of its history. Beams start out of plasterwork. Finely-turned staircases appear and disappear. Upstairs is a glorious display of miniature carpentry, pottery and needlework. Much of it needs a magnifying glass.

Ormesby hall

 An 18th-century house with modern paintings

At Ormesby, 3 miles SE of Middlesbrough; National Trust, open part year

The Pennymans' Ormesby estate was all but destroyed by 'the wicked Sir James' in the 1770s. Inheriting the house built by his uncle in the 1740s, he became an MP, mayor of Beverley, racing fanatic and gambler. He had Carr of York design lavish stables at Ormesby, and died bankrupt in 1808.

Somehow the family rescued the estate. His descendants lived in the house, with increasing forbearance, until 1983. The last occupant, Ruth Pennyman, staged Shakespeare in the stables and offered rehearsal space for Joan Littlewood's theatre troupe. Ormesby passed to the National Trust in 1961.

The house adorns an otherwise bleak corner of Teesside. It is reached across a park thankfully freed of the noisy sprawl of Middlesbrough, and stands four square and rather forbidding, its stone yellow-green with lichen. The chief feature of the hall and reception rooms is the remarkable plasterwork commissioned by Lady Pennyman (Sir James's aunt) in the 1740s. Scallops and wood-carving

surround pictures recently collected by the last Mrs Pennyman, including modern and abstract works.

The dining room has the finest ceiling in the house, a *trompe-l'œil* work of the 1770s. The pictures are mostly copies, of the sort often made when the originals have been sold to make ends meet. They are preferable to none. The Den beyond contains a rare collection of estate maps on rollers.

Ormesby's upstairs gallery is formed from what is, in essence, a landing and a corridor running across the centre of the house. The doors to the bedrooms are each decorated with different grades of ornament, depending on the importance of the room. This subtle architectural class distinction embellishes the most notable space in the house.

Richmond castle

⭐ A Norman keep and Victorian army barracks with detention cells

At Richmond; English Heritage, open all year

Richmond's huge walls of masonry, dating from the Norman Conquest, tower over a wooded bend in the River Swale. This is the site of the Great Hall of the Earls of Richmond. The D-shaped courtyard beyond was large enough to protect all the townspeople in time of attack. At the town side of this courtyard rises the Norman keep, in remarkably good repair. Outside is the market place, commerce and castle in happy proximity.

Although the Great Hall, known as Scolland's Hall after Earl Alan's steward, is a walled ruin, the tower keep survives, a fine remnant of Norman military architecture dating from the mid-12th century. Walls are still square and of great thickness. The plan is simple. A ground floor for storage and a well are accessible only from above. The next floor contains a large chamber probably used by soldiers. Above that is the principal chamber of the castle constable. Stairs and smaller chambers are built into the width of the walls.

The roof walk offers fine views over Swaledale. The castle was used as an army barracks in the 19th century, most of the buildings having since been removed. A series of detention cells survive. They housed conscientious objectors during the Great War when death sentences were commuted to hard labour. The cells still have graffiti by these prisoners, testament to one of the British Army's less edifying episodes.

Left Among those conscripted during World War I, there were many who were not prepared to 'take the King's shilling' and join the army. Usually pacifists, they were known as conscientious objectors and were punished by imprisonment and hard labour. One such prisoner of conscience held at Richmond Castle was Percy Goldsbrough, who left this message on his cell wall.

Rievaulx abbey

★ ★ A picturesque Cistercian ruin

At Rievaulx, 2 miles NW of Helmsley;
English Heritage, open all year

Rievaulx is the best surviving relic of the
Cistercian colonization of North Yorkshire in
the 12th century. Its surrounding hills and glades
came to embody the subsequent cult of English
Picturesque. The founder in 1132 (two years
before the start of Fountains Abbey, see page 54)
was William, secretary to the order's presiding
genius, St Bernard of Clairvaux. He was invited
here by Walter Espec, Lord of Helmsley, who
shared Henry I's religious zeal. The Rievaulx
community rapidly expanded, embracing
640 monks and lay-brothers at its peak.

The ruins are those of a monastery in the
Early Gothic style. Rievaulx church saw one of
the first pointed arches in England, the masons

presumably imported from Burgundy. The
residential quarters are as fine as those of
Fountains, but more complex. Nothing like it
in its full glory can have been seen in Northern
Europe since Roman times, certainly nothing in
Yorkshire. To the Saxon and Viking inhabitants,
this building on the wooded banks of the River
Rye must have seemed utterly awe-inspiring.

The refectory survives complete, almost to
roof height. Six lavers or washing places flank
its north door. Early English windows are
interspersed with blind arcading, decorated
with shafts. Here the monks ate in silence,
listening to readings from the pulpit. Less
complete but still impressive is the dormitory.

Next to it are the ruins of the abbot's house,
converted by Abbot Burton into reputedly one
of the largest such residences in England.
It included a Long Gallery and the usual private
chambers of a Tudor dignitary. A late Gothic
window survives with, above it, a relief of the
Annunciation in alabaster. The old Infirmary
Cloister was converted into the Abbot's private
garden. These quarters were still being built at
great expense during Rievaulx's final decline.

Rievaulx terrace Ionic temple

⭐ Banqueting hall in a picturesque landscape

At Rievaulx, 2 miles NW of Helmsley; National Trust, open part year

The picturesque quality of the Rievaulx Terrace has long been regarded as supreme in England. The second Thomas Duncombe of Duncombe Park (see page 52) treated the Abbey ruins as the most 'Heaven-sent' of landscape features. They were a foil for this classical mansion, located a mile distant in a secluded valley of the River Rye. Here in 1758 Duncombe laid out a terrace with a temple at either end. Between them runs a serpentine alley from which sudden views were cut through the trees to the ruins below. One temple was circular and Doric, a rotunda, the other rectangular, Ionic.

The Ionic Temple is a banqueting house. The interior is one large room, immaculately designed in the style of William Kent and well restored by the National Trust. It has a deeply coved ceiling based on one in the Palazzo Farnese in Rome. The coving copies Farnese motifs by Annibale Carracci. The ceiling above is by Giovanni Borgnis, a copy of a Guido Reni at the Casino Rospigliosi. Italy has come to Yorkshire in style, architecture massaged into landscape. A broken pediment crowns the marble fireplace. There are two grand Kentian settees in heavy giltwood, and the table is laid out for dinner.

'Italy has come to Yorkshire in style'

Above and left The Rievaulx Terrace and its temples were built by the second Thomas Duncombe of Duncombe Hall. His father had created a similar terrace nearer to the hall which offered views over Helmsley Castle. The ruins of both Helmsley and Rievaulx were part of the Duncombe estate and the Thomases made the most of their picturesque qualities. A visitor walking along the curving Rievaulx Terrace can see 13 different views of Ryedale and the Abbey. Although these vistas appear natural, they were in fact completely contrived, created by cutting through the trees and landscaping the surrounding woodland.

Right The Knight's Chamber is home to a range of different arms and armour, including items from the Civil War era. The Ingilby family sided with the King during this conflict and were prepared to bear arms in his support. Probably the most notable Ingilby soldier was 'Trooper Jane', a daughter of the family who enlisted in the Royalist army. It is claimed that she held Oliver Cromwell prisoner for a night in the castle's library.

Ripley castle

★ ★ ★ Tudor tower house with Georgian mansion attached

At Ripley, 3½ miles N of Harrogate; private house and gardens, open all year

In 1355 Thomas Ingilby was lucky enough to rescue Edward III from a menacing boar. He was knighted and richly rewarded. Twenty-six generations of Ingilbys have occupied this site ever since. Their boar's head device is everywhere, in the village, church and inn. Ingilby history drips from every wall and gazes from every portrait. The guidebook to the castle is 32 pages long, 22 of them devoted to the doings of the family. They clearly mean to stay.

The castle's most striking aspect is from across the lake, on which it appears to float like a magic tableau. The approach from the village is more severe. The walls are intact and the 1450s gatehouse impressive. On its inner side is where Cromwell's troops executed Royalist soldiers after Marston Moor, the stones still pitted with their shot. Across the court are two ranges, the Old Tower of 1555 and the main house rebuilt in the 1780s by William Belwood, a protégé of Robert Adam. The castle is today run as part residence, part business, curiously described by the owner as a 'coral reef'. On my last visit, it was crowded with Peugeot salesmen and driving simulators. Good luck to them.

Over a door in the entrance hall is a picture of Edward III and above it the head of the celebrated boar, source of the family's

Left Edward III in a portrait displayed in the entrance hall at Ripley. Edward came to the throne in 1327, when he was just 15 years old, and ruled England until 1377. Among the achievements of his reign was the medieval palace he had built at Windsor Castle. Thomas Ingilby's brother, Henry, played an important part in the project; he was charged by the King to collect taxes to help fund the building work.

blessings. The Georgian dining room recalls the many Ingilbys who have served their nation in war and on film and television. Ripley's credits must be the longest of any English house, from 'Jane Eyre' to 'Frankenstein'; the current Lady Ingilby has appeared on television with 'handy hints' on how to clean chandeliers with a hose.

The 16th-century Old Tower contains three chambers, one on each floor. The library, sadly short of books, is dark with rich panelling and old portraits. Despite siding with Edward III against the boar, the Ingilbys were otherwise on the 'wrong' side of history. Devout Catholics, they were implicated in the Gunpowder Plot and joined Prince Rupert's army during the Civil War, a daughter enlisting as 'Trooper Jane'. They lost their fortune and almost their lives. They then sided with James II and had to flee the country in 1688.

The upper landing is lit by a fine Venetian window filled with armorial stained glass,

depicting sixteen generations of Ingilbys. The Tower Room is panelled from floor to plasterwork ceiling, with emblems celebrating James I's procession from Scotland in 1603, when he seems to have stopped at every house in the North. The room was especially decorated for his stay.

At the top of the Old Tower is the Knight's Chamber, with original oak ceiling and a collection of ancient armour and weapons, including Cromwellian boots and shoes. The room carries the arms of Queen Mary and King Philip, rare in English houses given the brevity (and unpopularity) of their joint reign. The room contains some of the finest pictures in the house, including one of Elizabeth I. She, at least, ensured glory for one family member, the Blessed Francis Ingilby, whom she martyred in 1586. He was beatified in 1987. Although no longer Catholic, the family went to Rome for the ceremony.

House of correction

★ Example of Victorian penal system

St Marygate, Ripon; museum, open part year

The town of Ripon has what it calls a 'Law and Order Trail'. This includes a lock-up, police cells, courthouse, debtors prison, house of correction and workhouse, all from the 19th century or earlier. Nothing is too grim for modern tourism. The original 17th-century house of correction was for the 'correction of vagabonds and sturdy beggars', but the severity of the punishment, including whipping and hard labour, was clearly no deterrent (or correction) since the magistrates constantly needed more room. A new prison block was built in 1816 and remained in use into the 1950s.

Here the prisoners lived two to a cell, men and women segregated, with eight cells in all. Food was carefully regulated, as was the hard labour on a treadmill in the yard, yet the parish authorities ensured that prisoners worshipped daily and were taught to read if illiterate. They rarely spent more than short periods incarcerated. Only one person in fifty years was known to have died in the prison.

The cells are now used mostly for an exhibition of Ripon policing, including displays of whipping and flogging and the history of handcuffs. But one cell is furnished as it was in the 1860s, with simple plank, mug, plate and Bible, and a prisoner in uniform. He also has a punishment 'crank', whereby he had to turn a handle connected to a rod in sand outside the wall. Screw adjustments made this labour harder or easier, giving rise to the term 'screw' for prison warder.

Right In 1877 Ripon Workhouse opened its vagrants' wing, or casuals' ward. This was where tramps and other homeless itinerants could get a meal and a bed for the night in return for labour, usually chopping wood or breaking rocks. Before they could eat or take to their beds, however, vagrants had to wash in the bathhouse while their clothes were taken to be fumigated. The casuals' ward was in use until around 1960, although by then it was known as a 'wayfarer's reception centre'.

Left Today, the 'crank' may seem to be a very pointless punishment; the prisoner laboured but with no end result. However, in the 19th century, there was a popular belief that 'the devil makes work for idle hands'. This ethic was so strong that, to many Victorian minds, any man who worked hard was morally superior to one who did not. Therefore, labour, whether it had an end product or not, became an important part of punishment and redemption.

Union workhouse

⭐ Rare surviving Poor House

Allhallowgate, Ripon; museum, open part year

'Hush-a-bye baby, on a tree top, When you grow old, your wages will stop, When you have spent the little you made, First to the poorhouse and then to the grave.'

'Hush-a-bye baby, on a tree top,/ When you grow old, your wages will stop,/ When you have spent the little you made,/ First to the poorhouse and then to the grave.' Thus ran the rhyme that greeted new inmates to the workhouse. In 1832, the Ripon institution had thirty-three of all ages and genders. An inspection led to reform and expansion.

A new workhouse was built in 1854, with master and matron, treasurer and doctor. There were eventually separate wards and exercise areas for men and women, a vegetable garden, infirmary and even nursery. Everything, including the daily diet, was prescribed by the Board of Guardians. This was not so much a mini-welfare state as a civic kibbutz. At Christmas there was a special dinner and the mayoress sang to the inmates, accompanied by the vicar on the piano.

The Ripon Workhouse is one of the few such residential compounds to survive. The master's house and main wards have been converted for use by the local social services department. The 1877 vagrants' wing remains in its original form and is open as a museum. This is where those 'of no fixed abode' would be rounded up, washed, given an evening meal and a task to earn their keep – and told to leave the next morning.

Visitors are greeted with the smell of carbolic soap from the adjacent decontamination bathhouse. Next door is the eating room with a list of prescribed ingredients and a stove. Inmates could insist on a proper diet. Beyond are the 14 night cells. The exercise yard outside has its spikes pointing inwards to prevent escape before the required regime had been completed. With the advent of the welfare state, the poorhouse cells were briefly converted into 'rooms', with flowers, curtains and open doors.

RYEDALE

Ryedale folk museum

At Hutton-le-Hole,
8 miles NW of Pickering;
open part year

This museum contains some of England's best vernacular buildings. The houses are not left empty but are imaginatively furnished and benefit from being set behind the village in a field leading up onto the open moor as if a street. All are original cottages, although the Crofter's Cottage is re-created from fragments.

Crofter's cottage ✳

I did not know there were English crofts. This is a re-creation of the museum's poorest habitation. It is a single chamber, as existed from the 13th century to the end of the Middle Ages. Two beds occupy one end, a fireplace the middle and animals the other. The fire is kept burning. Smoke fills the roof. The shack contains the tools and utensils of the period, pots and sacks hanging from the rafters. The place needs animals and smells.

The beds are remarkably warm and comfortable, according to the custodian who has slept on one. The hardness of country life is often stressed by historians and archaeologists. It is refreshing to see that make-do-and-mend could also yield a convenient and self-sufficient home in which misery was not necessarily dominant.

Harome cottage ✳ originally at Harome, SE of Helmsley

This cottage came from Harome in the 1970s and has been restored to its condition as at the end of the 19th century. The structure is cruck-framed and very old. It still has 'opposing doors' at the kitchen end so a through draft could blow away the chaff when the floor was being used for threshing. The house is stone-built with a steep, thatched roof. The windows have Yorkshire sashes which slide sideways. Inside are now three rooms, the kitchen, with a range of dried fruit and herbs, a downstairs bedroom and a sitting room. There are more bedrooms upstairs, privacy being the chief 19th-century innovation for the poor. The house is fully furnished and a fire burns in the range. It seems a pity nobody lives here. The cottage has its own garden, planted with lavender, columbine, leopard's-bane, Jacob's ladder and primula.

Manor house

⭐ originally at Harome, SE of Helmsley

This is a grander affair, also brought from Harome. Formerly called Harome Hall, it was on the Helmsley estate of the Duncombes, Earls of Feversham, where surely it could have been retained. The structure is again cruck-framed, but the crucks are massive and repeated, with tie-beams to support the roof and stone walls. In its early medieval form, it would have offered a large communal chamber, the lord and his servants sleeping and eating together.

By the 16th century, one end had been partitioned with timbers, wattle and daub. The hall would later have had a complete upper floor inserted. This has been removed, leaving only the lord's upper chamber, or solar, at one end as his private room, with wood block stairs up to it. The house is used for exhibitions, depriving it of much of its character.

Left The roof at the Manor House is supported by massively impressive oak crucks, set in pairs that meet at the apex of the roof to form a series of inverted Vs. Each pair of crucks is linked by two beams, the collar-beam above and the tie-beam below.

Stang End cruck house

⭐ originally at Danby, 14m W of Whitby

So picturesque are these early structures that it is hard to imagine, let alone recreate, the poverty they concealed. This house is a 15th-century cottage from Danby on the North York Moors, moved here in 1967. The construction is a simple cruck on stone footings, with a steep roof thatched with heather. Before partitioning, it would have been just one room, which the family shared with their cattle when the latter needed shelter. Later it was partitioned and, later still, given an upper floor for bedrooms and storage. The upper floor has been removed.

The house is thus presented in its intermediate, partitioned form. There is a living room at one end with a salt-and-spice box and a rare witch-post to ward off evil. The centre space is taken up with a milk-and-cheese house, for the making of Danby cheese. At the far end is a rough bedroom with a spinning wheel. The house is furnished on the basis of an old inventory.

Above These carved lines indicate Stang End's witch-post, which was believed to help to protect the house from witches. It also supports a smokehood over the fire.

RYEDALE

Scampston hall

★★ Regency mansion with interiors by Thomas Leverton

At Scampston, 5 miles NE of Malton; private house and gardens, open part year

Never judge a house by its face. Scampston from the main road is forbidding, a well-proportioned Regency villa rendered the colour of gunmetal. Who, having pondered stucco or limewash, could have chosen grey? Yet Scampston is grey and means to stay that way.

Grey the interiors are not. The house was remodelled in 1800 for the St Quintin family by the London architect Thomas Leverton (designer of Bedford Square). The plan is ingenious, with two fronts, an entrance and a longer façade to the garden. Both are enlivened by large bow windows. The house is surrounded by a formal parterre, the eye gliding easily into the park and to a graceful Palladian bridge over the lake.

The entrance is into a stone hall warmed by pale salmon walls and a battery of family portraits. To one side is a sitting room, with small landscapes by Samuel Scott. There is also a picture of an open book, the only case I know of painting thus deferring to literature. On the other side of the hall is the drawing room, turning the house along the garden axis. This was redecorated in the 1860s and retains carpets, curtains and wallpaper sparkling with mica from that period. On the wall is a Gainsborough landscape.

The library is the best room at Scampston. Marbled pilasters and attached columns frame the bow window, while the bookshelves are recessed into the walls under Soanian arches. The pictures, mostly by Gainsborough, are particularly well placed in the bow. Beyond is the dining room which, like the drawing room, is of exceptional width for a small private house. It is heavier in style and hung with an array of St Quintin baronets.

The staircase hall is Leverton at his best. As in his Bedford Square town houses (and as with Robert Adam), he had a talent for creating splendour in confined spaces.

The St Quintin family continue to occupy Scampston under the name of Legard. Its reclamation is largely the effort of the present Lady Legard, a historic buildings enthusiast, in the 1990s.

Right In the Library, the marbled pilasters framing the bow window have been painted to match two scagliola columns that were part of a decorative scheme from around 1800. **Below** The walled garden is a more recent innovation. Covering 4½ acres, it was designed by Chelsea-medal winner, Piet Oudolf. Within the original walls, the garden has been divided up with beech hedges to create a number of 'rooms', each with a different look. Limes have been planted around three sides of the garden, up against the original wall. At one end is a grass-covered pyramid which offers a complete view of the garden, in imitation of a 17th-century 'prospect mound'.

Settle the folly

High Street, Settle; part museum (open part year), part private house (holiday let)

English architecture in the 17th century was rarely dull. In 1679 a wealthy Settle merchant named Richard Preston built himself a town house overlooking the market place. We assume he told his builder to give him big rooms, large fireplaces and a grand staircase, with some novelties so as not to look old-fashioned. Preston soon sold the house to a man named Dawson, whose descendants owned it for three centuries. By the 18th century it was no longer a house but a commercial building and was divided into two. The Dawson family sold it in 1980 and the main portion has now been opened as a museum.

Most remarkable is the exterior, covered in Jacobean motifs of the sort a local builder might have in his pattern book. The doorway is clearly a figment of his imagination. Two Gothicky arches beneath a squared hood are framed by two columns that are more Burmese than British, with mini-stupas on top. To the right are the mullioned windows of the old Great Hall. These continue across the recessed central bay of the house and round the projecting bay to the right. This handling of windows round a corner is more Bauhaus than 17th century, although it is reminiscent of Astley Hall (Lancashire). What

Above Classic architectural ornaments were distorted by The Folly's builder to create this extraordinary doorway with a distinctly oriental feel. The columns narrow towards their tops then flare out again to form wide, heavy capitals. The arches are positively Moorish in shape.

is surprising is that the mullions can carry the weight of the walls and roof above. Similar fenestration adorns the upper two floors.

Inside, the fireplaces are huge, as are the rooms themselves. The hall fireplace takes up almost the whole of one side, while the back wall is composed mostly of the stairwell. The staircase has twisted balusters and strange pilasters on the newel posts. It rises two storeys with generous treads, the sort of staircase normal in a grand house with space to spare. The rooms desperately need matting, tapestries and furniture, and why not a shop on the ground floor? The name of the house is obscure, probably because a good use could never be found for it.

Shandy hall

★★ Final home and shrine of Laurence Sterne

At Coxwold, 7 miles SW of Helmsley;
private house and garden, open part year

Laurence Sterne was an impecunious vicar
who earned fame and fortune with the
publication of his comic novel, *Tristram
Shandy*, in 1760. In that year, he acquired
the living of Coxwold where he lived until his
death in 1768. Although a modest cottage,
it was immediately dubbed Shandy Hall.
Here Sterne continued to write and, after
being abandoned by his wife, to recover from
falling in love with the twenty-three-year-old
Eliza Draper.

After Sterne's death, Shandy Hall became
a farmhouse. It was near derelict when a
trust was established in 1967 to restore it as
a shrine to the writer and as a home for the
honorary curators, the Monkmans, who
occupied it until recently. A full time curator
is now in residence. The house is a brick-
covered cottage, guarded by holly trees.
Gabled cross-wings on either side of the old
hall are flanked in turn by a massive kitchen
chimney to the right and by Sterne's
Georgian extension to the left.

The inside is cosy. The parlour/kitchen
has an 18th-century range and decorated
bread oven door. The beamed study contains
a library of Sterniana, evocative of a literary
clergyman. The dining room is on the site
of what would have been the Great Hall,
oak-panelled and painted, with Shandy prints
and pictures on the walls. Most enjoyable
is Sterne's sitting room. It is the nearest the
place comes to grandeur. He called it one of
the 'elegant touches to my Shandy Castle'.

Right Sterne's study at Shandy Hall. Today, the book
shelves are home to a unique collection of first and
early editions of his writings. Open on the table are
works by authors who would have influenced Sterne,
including Shakespeare, Cervantes and Montaigne.
Three portraits of Sterne hang above the fireplace.

The delightful gardens of Shandy Hall provide the perfect setting for Sterne's very personal home. Although the house was rented, from the Fauconberg Estate, Sterne made many additions and alterations to suite his taste – the view here shows the brick front he added as part of a scheme to 'gentrify' the property.

Laurence Sterne
1713–1768

Sterne was born in Clonmel in Ireland, where his army-officer father was stationed. At the age of 10 he went to live with a relative in Yorkshire, who sent him to school in Halifax. At 20 he arrived at Cambridge on a scholarship, and a career in the church followed. In 1738 he obtained the living at Sutton-on-the-Forest near York, where he began to build a reputation for his sermons. Success with the first volume of *Tristram Shandy* coincided with his move to Coxwold. It also brought him fame in London society – his portrait (above) was painted by Joshua Reynolds. Sterne died in London in 1768 and was buried at Bayswater, but two days later his remains were stolen by body snatchers. His body turned up in an anatomy lecture in Cambridge, where fortunately someone recognised his face and he was returned to his grave. In 1969 his bones were exhumed once more, for re-burial at Coxwold.

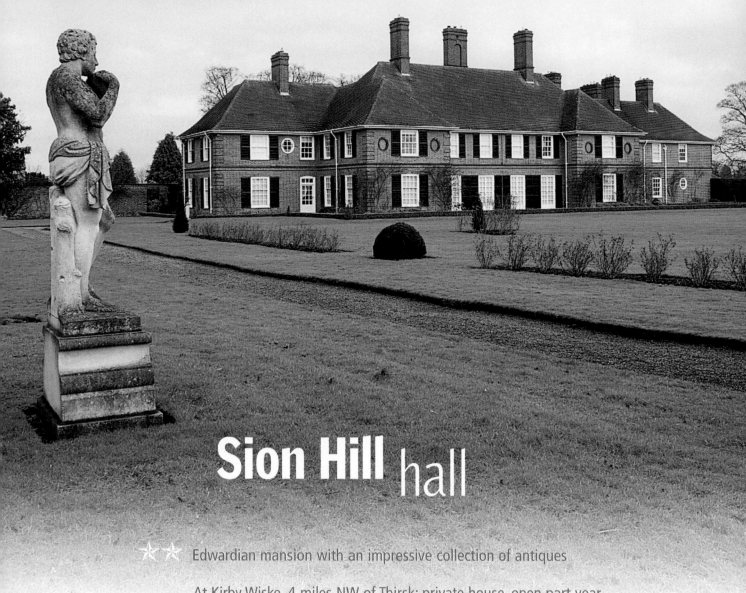

Sion Hill hall

✶✶ Edwardian mansion with an impressive collection of antiques

At Kirby Wiske, 4 miles NW of Thirsk; private house, open part year

Sion Hill is a monument to the antique collector as addict. A century of assiduous buying and selling has shown that a good eye and a keen ear for a bargain can amass in a few decades what it would take a public museum centuries to acquire. The present incumbent is Michael Mallaby. He inherited the responsibility for Sion Hill Hall from Herbert Mawer, a Yorkshire businessman who bought it in 1962 and filled it with antiques. These were mostly of French furniture and china. Eager to keep the house and collection together as a memorial to his endeavour, Mawer put them into a trust, with Mr Mallaby in occupation and in charge.

The house was built in 1913 by Walter Brierley of York for Percy Stancliffe, on the ruins of a decayed Georgian mansion belonging to the Lascelles family. Brierley was dubbed the 'Lutyens of the North'. His low spreading manor house is in that architect's style, redbrick of two storeys with steep hipped roofs and tall assertive chimneys. The house is fine, even if the details lack the flair and humour of the master.

The reception rooms are laid out along a spinal corridor the length of the ground and first floors. These corridors are modulated by keystoned arches and warmed by the dark reds and blues with which Mr Mallaby has decorated them. The rooms follow a formal sequence of breakfast room, dining room, drawing room and library. The style is rich and crowded, sometimes Curzon Street Baroque, sometimes antique

Above Sion Hill starts as it means to go on – the main entrance is packed with antiques. Fine pieces of furniture line the ground floor hall, statues and busts stand on plinths, clocks and paintings hang from the walls. The furniture includes two heavily carved German chairs, dating from the 19th century, and a magnificent late 17th-century Italian cabinet. The large classical busts depict Nero and Faustinia. **Below** Smaller curiosities and collectables have a place at Sion Hill too. The glass pig gin decanter, with a stopper as its snout, is Dutch; the bee-shaped honey pot beside it was made by Mappin and Webb in the early 1900s.

dealer's Louis XVI. Surfaces are so crowded that there is scarcely room to place a champagne cooler or copy of *Country Life*.

Yet no inch is without thought or interest. A honey pot is in the form of a bee. A gin decanter is in the form of a pig. At every turn is a case of Meissen, a shelf of Crown Derby, a cabinet of Worcester. Mr Mallaby is a clock specialist and the house is alive with ticking and chiming. The old kitchen has been restored with much burnished copper and is in regular use as a dining room.

Skipton castle

★ ★ ☆   Clifford stronghold with a medieval inner court

At Skipton, 20 miles W of Harrogate; private house and grounds, open all year

Skipton's Market Place leads joyfully uphill to Skipton Castle. The pink-and-black gatehouse bursts with medieval self-confidence. The outer bailey is picturesque rather than forbidding, a good place for a picnic, but the seven towers of the inner castle are daunting. Two of them glare down on the sole entrance below, like thuggish bouncers challenging any attempt on the door. On the far side, the walls drop to the ravine of the Eller Beck.

The entrance itself is oddly delicate. Its oriel window was apparently the 17th-century insertion of Anne Clifford, whose family had held Skipton since 1310. She assiduously restored and fenestrated the castles in her custodianship, in defiance of her foe, Oliver Cromwell (see Barden Tower, page 33). Inside is the delightful medieval Conduit Court, surrounded by walls, towers, windows and doors. It is a miniature version of the old court at Berkeley (Gloucestershire). An ancient yew planted by Lady Anne presides over its centre. Steps rise to the Great Hall.

The undoubted magic of Conduit Court partly evaporates as we explore the interior. Although intact and roofed, the rooms are all bare, scraped, scrubbed and restored. Beams are exposed everywhere and walls covered in whitewash. This smacks of English Heritage corporate identity, odd since the house is privately owned. There is no distinction between any of the chambers and little indication of their use. Most are empty.

Above A medieval visitor to Skipton Castle would have crossed the moat, and then passed under the portcullis and through the main doors before reaching Conduit Court. A close inspection of some of the walls in the courtyard reveals several small, incised marks. These are the initials or symbols of the various stone masons who worked on the building. By marking the stones they had dressed, each mason could ensure payment for the work he had done.

On the ground floor are former cellars, ancient cobbled guardrooms and worn steps to fighting platforms and dungeons. The first floor includes the Great Hall, kitchens, bedchambers and an impressive watchtower. In the East Tower is a Shell Room with tableaux showing the deities of Fire, Air, Water and Earth, ascribed to Isaac de Caus.

The best way to appreciate Skipton is to choose a day with few crowds and wander the rooms and battlements at random, leaving the imagination to do the work. The view from any of the chambers down onto the courtyard on a sunny day is blissful. Surely something can give these stones some life.

Stockeld park

 Vanbrughian-revival house designed by James Paine

2 miles NW of Wetherby; private house and grounds, open by arrangement only

This house does not wear its heart on its sleeve. It is reached across an extensive park outside Wetherby. The old part of the house is in a pink-grey ashlar, with millstone grit for the Victorian extension. The façade is unwelcoming, a heavy porch having been added in 1885.

Yet the main part of the house, by James Paine in 1758, hugely excited Pevsner as a work of what he called the Vanbrughian revival. The rooms received external expression, not concealed within a formal Palladian box. Wings are thrust forward from the central hall, with pediments and arched bays of their own. This is truly a ghost of Seaton Delaval (Northumberland).

The chief interest of the interior is the staircase, to which the word Baroque can again be applied. It is reached from Paine's entrance hall, with fine plasterwork round the doors. The staircase rises three storeys, the height of the house. It is cantilevered within an oblong volume, every feature of which reflects curvature. The architect is conductor of the interior, with doors and windows his orchestra. Each floor has semi-circular niches, within which are two curved doorways apiece. Seen from below, this creates a sense of mystery.

The other rooms have been much altered, although the dining room is still evidently Paine's, curved at each end. The house's owners, the Grant family, have recently redecorated the reception rooms in bold colours, a practice that seems appropriate where Georgian interiors are in need of a lift.

Left The hall, landings and soaring staircase at Stockeld Park combine in a symphony of curves. Decorative detail and classical ornament are used to emphasize the sinuous shapes of the architecture – even the banisters supporting the handrail bow gently outwards.

Sutton park

At Sutton-on-the-Forest, 8 miles N of York; private house and gardens, open part year

The Sheffield family goes in the male line back to the 13th century. Variously Earls of Mulgrave and Dukes of Buckingham, they are now back to baronets. In 1963, the family decided to vacate their seat at Normanby (Lincolnshire) and buy the smaller Sutton Park. It is a charming small Georgian house with none of the aloofness of Regency architecture. Sutton was also blessed by the stucco work of Joseph Cortese.

The exterior is plain, of *c*1745, with a single wide pediment embracing the entire five-bay façade. This is offset by flanking wings and, on the garden front, a bold frontispiece with a French window. The interiors are exquisite. The entrance hall is screened from the stairs by

Right The panelled walls of the Tea Room at Sutton Park have been painted to imitate tortoiseshell, with ivory details. Tortoiseshell was a popular material in the 18th century and was used to decorate many items, but to have covered a whole room with tortoiseshell would have been prohibitively expensive, hence the paint effect used here. The plates on the walls are Imari porcelain imported from Japan some time in the 1720s.

Corinthian columns beneath a Rococo ceiling by Cortese. This runs continuously from the door across the hall and up the stairs. The composition is enhanced by pale yellow walls and a stone floor. Waves and fronds billow from the depths of Cortese's imagination.

Sutton's reception rooms have benefited from imports from other houses, each with a distinct personality. The library has another Cortese ceiling, if anything finer than that in the hall. It is like a basket of flowers tied up with endless ribbons. The morning room has pine panelling worthy of a palace. It was made by Henry Flitcroft for a house in Leeds. Fluted pilasters run from floor to cornice line. The panels between them seem designed to frame the pictures they contain. One is a fine Holbein copy.

The Tea Room walls are painted in imitation tortoiseshell and have a display of Japanese porcelain while the adjacent Porcelain Room has Meissen and Chelsea. The Chinese Drawing Room, on a grander scale than the others, loses the visitor in a delicate oriental forest of Chinese wallpaper. Here is a Smirke fireplace from Normanby, a walnut bureau from old Buckingham House in London (also a one-time Sheffield property) and a dazzling Rococo mirror, complete with Ho-Ho bird.

The dining room was restored after the Second World War by Francis Johnson and is one of his happiest works. The leather screen came from an Armada ship.

Left Although contemporary to Sutton Park, the pine panelling that lines the Morning Room was originally made for Potternewton Hall in Leeds by the joiner-turned-architect, Henry Flitcroft. Above the fireplace hangs a portrait of the Earl of Wiltshire in the style of Holbein. **Right** The bookcases in the Library were brought by the Sheffields from the family's original home at Normanby Park in Lincolnshire. They are by Robert Smirke, the architect of both Normanby and the British Museum. The collection now on their shelves includes many first editions of important books.

Swinton park

★ ★ An aristocratic Victorian mansion

At Swinton, 6 miles S of Bedale;
now a hotel

When I first visited Swinton on a dark winter evening in the early 1970s, it seemed the sort of place in which the Victorians imprisoned their daughters for safe keeping before marriage. The elderly Earl of Swinton was being perambulated by his butler up and down gaunt corridors. Guests arriving, as I was, for occasional conferences in the house, would inhabit vast, cold reception rooms.

The original house was built in the 1690s but was never left in peace. It was altered by Carr of York in 1764 and further enlarged at the end of the 18th century and the beginning of the 19th. It was further extended by the 19th-century Lord Masham, described by John Cornforth as a 'gigantic Victorian of fantastic energy and compelling vigour'. Swinton is of Disraelian gloom and grandeur, castellated, mildly romantic, and now a luxury hotel.

The house is on rising ground on the outskirts of the village. A drive through fine gates and lodges reveals a large tower set over the entrance, with an L-shaped building beyond. The story of Swinton is of the progressive 'fortification' of both house and owner. The first Gothicizing was by Robert Lugar in 1821, working for William Danby. Lord Masham bought the house in 1882 and added storeys, wings, billiard room and library. He also raised the height of the tower; it looks like a fat man bursting out of his coat.

The hotel has retained the Victorian interiors, even at some expense of cosiness. The dining room has been restored, with gilded ceiling and heavy curtains. Family portraits and books still grace walls and bookshelves. The drawing room has a grand fireplace and bow window, possibly designed by James Wyatt. In an eccentric bar are comforting copies of the *Yorkshire Archaeological Journal*.

Thirsk: James Herriot's house

★ ★ Popular television vet's house and dispensary

23 Kirkgate, Thirsk; museum, open all year

The 'World of James Herriot' comes in three parts. First is the original home of the local Thirsk vet. Second is a television studio recreating the same house to the rear, as used in the series, *All Creatures Great and Small*. Third is a museum of veterinary science. Only the first concerns us here, although the others are first class of their kind.

James Herriot was the pen name of Alf Wight, a real vet. He moved to Thirsk in 1940 and joined the practice of Donald Sinclair, publishing his first volume of popular memoirs in 1970. He continued in practice until his death

in 1995. The house in which he lived and worked is Georgian, but the interiors have been restored to their 1950s appearance. This has been done with scholarship and wit. Wight was an enthusiast for clutter.

Downstairs, the dining room doubled as the office. There is also a sitting room, breakfast room, surgery and kitchen. Wight is depicted in effigy in the sitting room, but with his back to the door. Toys cover the floor, comics are everywhere and George Formby whines on the radio. The only living thing is a budgerigar. The dining room has a typewriter, copies of *The Lady* and *Tailwagger* and books from the Boots Circulation Library. An early black-and-white programme is playing on the television set.

Most extraordinary is the kitchen, portrayed at the moment of a Yorkshire tea. I have never seen artificial bacon and sausages look so real. The Herriot museum shows wax and plaster admirably employed to bring the past alive. The key is to do it well.

Above left The shelves in Wight's surgery at 23 Kirkgate are lined with bottles and packets that would have been filled with all sorts of medication for the different animals, 'great and small', that were treated at the practice.
Centre The comfortable domesticity of 1950s family life is perfectly preserved in the sitting room: a cat naps on an over-stuffed armchair; toys are strewn about; the figure on the right represents Wight himself, perusing his books..
Right The kitchen continues the 'lived-in' theme with a table set for traditional high tea. Linens hang from the airer above the stove, and baking utensils are left out on the oilcloth-covered side table as if cake-making is in progress.

James Herriot, aka Wight
1916-1995

James Alfred Wight, known as Alf, was born on 3rd October, 1916. Brought up in Glasgow, he graduated from the veterinary college there in 1939. He joined the veterinary practice in Thirsk in 1940, leaving it only for wartime service with the RAF and for occasional work abroad in the 1960s. He began writing in 1966 and in 1978 his first James Herriot novel, *All Creatures Great and Small*, was adapted for television. A second successful TV series ran from 1988 to 1990.

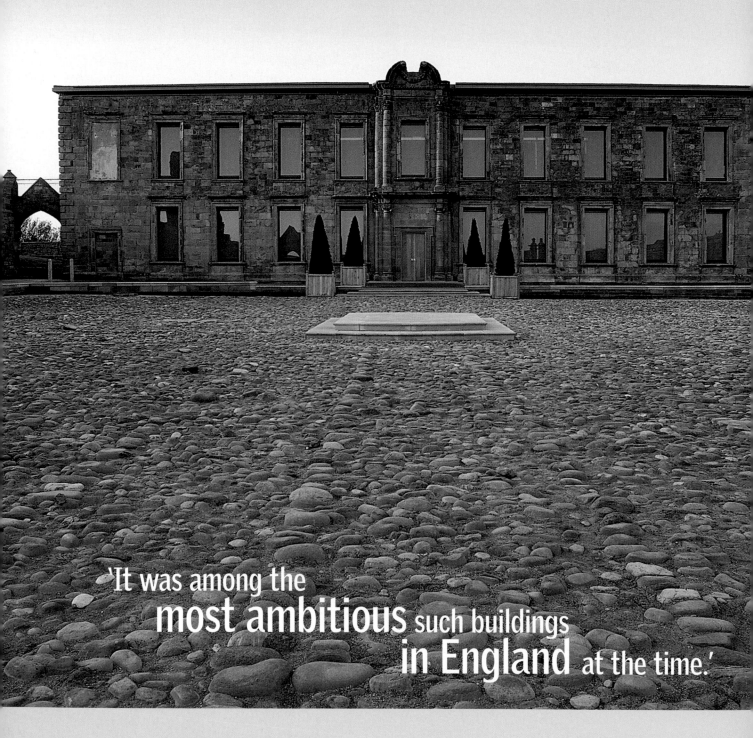

Whitby banqueting house

'It was among the
most ambitious such buildings
in **England** at the time.'

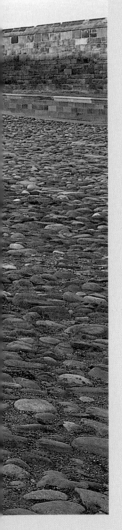

Above The ruins of Whitby Abbey still overshadow Sir Hugh Cholmley's Banqueting Hall (at top left in the photograph). Established in the 1070s, on the site of an earlier religious settlement, the Abbey was home to a monastic community until 1539. The remains of the 13th-century Abbey church dominate the local landscape from their prominent headland position overlooking Whitby harbour and the North Sea.

 Fantastical 17th-century façade, now modernized

At Whitby Abbey, on coast E of Whitby town; English Heritage, open all year

After the Dissolution of the Monasteries, Whitby Abbey on its cliff overlooking the town was acquired by the Cholmley family. They used the abbot's lodgings as a house and, in 1672, added a new banqueting house next door. This was clearly built for splendour rather than comfort and was rarely used. The building decayed and soon became derelict. No one who visited it on a bleak windy evening could doubt its inspiration as the English landfall of Bram Stoker's Count Dracula.

The massive façade is of 11 bays, with a fine Mannerist frontispiece flanked by columns and topped by an open pediment with garland. It was among the most ambitious such buildings in England at the time. Even ruined, the bricked-up windows had the silent assertiveness of their age. They marked the passage of time, while Whitby went about its business in the valley below.

They still do, but oh dear. I am in favour of reinstatement and admire the confidence with which Victorians went about rebuilding what were otherwise meaningless ruins. But English Heritage's 2002 work at Whitby Banqueting House is not reinstatement but a folly at the expense of a fine old building. The new Whitby visitor centre suggests a modern architect with no respect for the atmosphere and character of antiquity.

The windows have been replaced with cold plate glass. The walls have been stripped and scrubbed. The architects were clearly obsessed with imposing their favoured concrete, glass and steel, wholly alien materials, wherever they could. Ruining Whitby must have cost a fortune. To rub salt in the wounds, an actor dressed as 'Sir Hugh Cholmley' greets visitors to what is neither ancient nor modern. It is a warning of the fate which state ownership holds in store for all old buildings.

York

City

York City

Bar Convent museum

Below Now the main entrance hall to the Bar Convent, this spacious area was originally an open courtyard. It was enclosed in the 19th century with a glass roof. The colours of the bright Victorian tiles, **above right**, are repeated in the rich terracotta walls and blue marbled columns. Still home to a religious community, the Bar Convent is described as 'the oldest living convent in England'.

Above The convent Chapel, by Thomas Atkinson, was completed in 1769. Since Catholic worship was still forbidden at this time, the chapel was built at the heart of the convent to conceal it from general sight. Although the chapel is domed inside, outside the dome is hidden by a pitched roof in another piece of architectural subterfuge.

✶ Convent and Catholic centre within a Georgian town house

Blossom Street, York; museum, open part year

A reorganization of secondary schools in York in 1982 did away with the old Bar Convent School. It had been founded in 1686 by the 'Jesuitesses', an order of nuns of the Institute of the Blessed Virgin Mary. They were dedicated to what was almost unknown at the time, exclusively female education. The convent was much favoured by St Michael, whose sudden appearance miraculously saved it from destruction by an anti-Catholic mob in 1696.

The convent and school were rebuilt in 1787 as a pedimented Georgian town house, its chapel discreetly hidden across a small courtyard within. An adjacent extension, more ostentatious with larger windows and pilasters, was added in 1844.

Reorganization led the school to amalgamate with other Catholic schools at the rear of the site. The main buildings were converted for use as a museum, conference centre and 'bed & breakfast' for visiting groups. The convent still houses 10 active nuns and 10 retired. On the ground floor is the handsomely furnished Great Parlour where guests are greeted beneath portraits of benefactors and Superiors of the Order.

The Victorian extensions led to the courtyard being glazed, thus forming a charming winter garden. The bright floor tiles are from Coalbrookdale. Upstairs rooms offer a museum of the history of Christianity in York. Sometimes accessible are the library, with books on Catholic history, and the chapel, a rotunda supported by fluted Ionic columns, recently restored to its original Georgian appearance.

Below Painstaking study has been the basis for the Great Hall's restoration. The square hearth and floor tiles have been reconstructed based on archaeological evidence from the site. A wall-hanging has been created to decorate one of the walls; the colours used and the design, featuring the white rose of York, were inspired by a 15th-century Book of Hours.

Barley hall

⭐ Reconstruction of a medieval hall house

Coffee Yard, off Stonegate, York; museum, open all year

In the 1980s, archaeologists seeking a Roman house beneath a plumber's workshop hit the footings of the hall house of a former Lord Mayor of *c*1400. They stopped there and decided to reconstruct it.

The floor tiles and some of the timbers are original. The rest is a replica designed by the York Archaeological Trust, named after its founder, Maurice Barley. Given the opposition of most archaeologists to such reconstruction, the Trust and the York planning authority deserve all praise.

The site is a godsend to hard-pressed tour guides. It comprises a hall and two-storey solar range, thought to have belonged to Nostell Priory. The Great Hall is visible from a glass screens passage formed from what is a public alleyway. It is of two bays with roof trusses, balcony and lord's platform. The chamber is well crowded with new medieval furniture.

Having gone this far, I cannot see why the Trust does not go two steps further and re-create some of the mess, dirt, colour and rats of a medieval hall. They should take a leaf from the Jorvik book. Barley looks too much like a medieval kit.

Clifford's tower

★ Tower keep of the city's medieval castle

Tower Street, York; English Heritage, open all year

The tower is the keep of York's medieval castle. It sits atop its grassy motte within the old city walls, wholly dominating what is now York Castle Museum at its foot. The round bastions have subsided slightly, giving the walls an alarming outward tilt, but the building is intact and offers a fine view of the city from above.

The castle was built after the Norman Conquest and was an important fortress. The present keep was erected in 1244, by which time the old Norman square shape was outdated and round was 'in'. The quatrefoil plan is unique in England, supposedly based on the Château d'Étampes outside Paris. It was designed to give defenders the widest range of fire from the windows. The Clifford family were hereditary constables of York Castle. Locals nicknamed it the mince pie.

The entrance gateway, up 55 steep steps, is Jacobean and dated 1642, the last time the keep was garrisoned during the Civil War. Then in 1684 a spectacular fire destroyed most of the interior and left it a picturesque folly. The interior would have had two floors, supported by a massive central pier, the foot of which remains. There is a Gothic chapel above the gatehouse. The tower is a jolly place spoilt only by laboured English Heritage marketing.

'It is now again among the finest Georgian survivals in England.'

Left The stucco work at Fairfax House is among its greatest treasures. The plasterwork medallion high on the wall opposite the main staircase depicts Eternal Rome holding the winged figure of Victory. Three different roses hang from the base of the medallion, each with symbolic significance for the original Catholic owners of the house.

Fairfax house

★★★☆ Restored Georgian nobleman's town house

27 Castlegate, York; museum, open part year

Those who lament the loss of so many fine English town houses can take comfort from Fairfax House. All but a ruin in the 1920s, the building was used variously as a dance hall and a foyer and cloakroom to an adjacent cinema. It is now again among the finest Georgian survivals in England. Begun *c*1745 and fitted out for Viscount Fairfax *c*1755–62, it was created from the wealth of land and restored from the wealth of chocolate. The interior is the masterpiece of Carr of York, but it is also a masterpiece of restoration by Francis Johnson for the York Civic Trust in 1982–84. The rooms hold the Noel Terry collection of furniture, clocks and porcelain. They seem cold, watched over by spectral attendants, but that is a small price to pay for a feast.

The façade onto Castlegate is of five bays with a central pediment, the doorcase a handsome Doric. The interior of the ground floor survived years of abuse when there was a public dance hall and leaking lavatories above. Almost all the stucco is contemporary with the house and is English Rococo. The furniture is Georgian. The hall and staircase are a crescendo of Joseph Cortese's plasterwork, creating a maximum of impact inside a minimum of space. The stair rises to a Venetian window crowned with the Fairfax arms, returning to a landing flanked by magnificent Corinthian doorcases. Walls and ceiling are encrusted with Cortese's stuccowork. Palms and swags support busts of Newton and Shakespeare. The deeply coved ceiling is militaristic, with weapons, trophies, flags and putti holding a light for the 'true religion', Fairfax being a Roman Catholic.

Two superb rooms grace the first floor, the drawing room and the saloon. The drawing room ceiling has fronds embracing a depiction of Friendship. The walls are hung with green damask. The saloon plasterwork is the finest in the house. The foliage seems in perpetual motion, swirling across the ceiling towards a frieze of lions and leaves.

The Viscount's bedroom across the passage was rescued from use as a cinema lavatory. The bed is a four-poster designed by Francis Johnson himself. On it is laid a fine silk dressing-gown with velvet cuffs, together with a rosary and book of poems. Fairfax's daughter Anne's bedroom has vivid wallpaper in what is known as a Mock India pattern. A painting over the fireplace depicts her as a shepherdess.

The kitchen downstairs shows preparation for the Viscount's dinner on 15 April 1763. He ate well. The present entrance to Fairfax House is through an adjacent building. This is a pity since it denies proper access by the front door.

Jorvik Viking centre

★ ★ Enjoyable re-creation of Viking everyday life

Coppergate, York; museum, open part year

Archaeologists excavating what is now the Coppergate Shopping Centre in the early 1980s suddenly found themselves walking down what appeared to be a Viking street. It ran along the old bank of the River Ouse. They discovered not only a wealth of material but also wooden beams of original houses. The street was preserved beneath the modern building and the houses were carefully reconstructed *in situ*. Some new properties were added to create at least part of an authentic Viking settlement. York was a Norse-speaking city of 10,000 people in AD 975, less than a century before the Norman Conquest. The site is hugely popular.

Visitors to the centre are conveyed down the street in open cars on an overhead track. Countryside has been painted in the distance.

Two-storey houses of wood flank a street populated with animated figures, workers, merchants and fishwives, all chatting in Old Norse. A man sits on a primitive toilet.

At a point in the tour, the car swivels round and goes inside the biggest of the reconstituted houses, that of a leatherworker. In the car, the visitor rises from cellar to first floor, seeing storage casks in the former, and women and children working the leather above. Skins hang to dry inside the roof. Next door a man turns wooden cups on a small lathe, hence the 'cuppergate' or street of the makers of cups.

Jorvik is a good example of confident reconstruction of the past – by a private company – of a sort that public authorities seem unable to do. And it stinks – as old streets did.

Below Excavations at Coppergate in York unearthed many items made of leather preserved in remarkably good condition, as well as specialist tools such as awls, punches, needles and beeswax balls. The evidence indicated that leather boots and shoes were being both repaired and made at the site, along with belts, bags and even scabbards. This reconstruction of a leatherworker in action forms part of the visitor's tour.

The King's manor

✦ ✦ Abbey relics now housing a modern university

Behind Museum St, York; part of York university, courtyard open all year

St Mary's Benedictine abbey was the wealthiest monastic house in the north of England. Such was its prosperity and prominence that monks dissatisfied by its luxury deserted in 1132, joined the Cistercian Order and founded Fountains and Rievaulx abbeys to the north. We therefore have much for which to be thankful to the monks of St Mary's.

The present manorial buildings were the abbot's lodgings, seized by the Crown at the Dissolution to become the headquarters of the powerful Council of the North and residence of its President. It was here that the monarchs would stay on visits to the city.

The manor has re-established a sort of monastic heritage as York University. Next door are the old abbey ruins, where the York Mystery plays are still performed. While alteration has left few interiors of special merit, the ensemble is picturesque and not unlike an Oxford college.

The King's Manor is a place of doorways and openings. The approach to the main entrance is through a set of finely worked wrought-iron gates, **above**. In the middle of the Manor's main frontage is another doorway, **left**, constructed in the early 17th century and moved to this position after 1820. The door is surrounded by intricately carved stonework; the figures of Justice and Prudence are directly above the door. Inside the main courtyard stands another magnificent 17th-century doorway, **right**, this one supporting the arms of Thomas Wentworth, 1st Earl of Strafford.

'The **manor** has re-established a sort of **monastic heritage** ... picturesque and not unlike an **Oxford** college.'

The manor is round two courtyards, its pleasure derived from their various façades. Sixteenth- and early 17th-century frontispieces frame each doorway, often in crumbling form. Most of the ranges house the university's architecture and archaeology departments. For some reason, 'advanced architecture' is in a medieval block, medieval architecture in a modern one.

Entry is by the Postern Gate. The original block is a U-shaped medieval house of the late 15th century. This has a superb Jacobean doorway with pilasters, coat of arms and a high pediment. Passing into the courtyard, we see ranges, steps, windows and doors of all periods, built as and when required and to no overall plan. Since most of the interiors were sanitized when the university arrived in the early 1960s, a dreadful architectural era, there is little of interest inside. On the left is an old Hall, now a refectory, while on the right is the Council Chamber.

Mansion house

Below Among the grand reception rooms at York's Mansion House is the Dining Room on the ground floor. One of its chief attractions is the fabulous ceiling, covered with a relief decoration that stands as a monument to what can be achieved with wallpaper.

✫✫ Georgian mayoral residence

St Helen's Square, York; civic building, open part year

York is rightly proud of its Mansion House, claiming it as the only one in England in which the mayor actually lives during his or her year of office. (This is, however, true of London's Mansion House.) The city's ancient Guildhall lies behind. The house was completed in 1729, possibly by a local man, William Etty. The façade is simple, of stuccoed brick with colourful decoration and is very much the centre of attention in St Helen's Square.

To the left of the entrance hall is a large dining room running from the front to the back of the building. The ceiling looks like it has been made in stucco but is, in fact, wallpaper. The climax of the house is the progress to the main state room above. Arch, stairs and landings are crowded with gilded stucco.

The stairwell is dominated by a portrait of York's most controversial son, the 'railway king', George Hudson. He built the line from York to London and lived in the largest house in Belgravia, now the French Embassy. He went bankrupt, was accused of embezzlement and disgraced. The burghers of York scratched the name from his portrait, but could not bring themselves to take down the picture. (Doncaster Mansion House is shocked that York should decorate its stairs with such a man.)

Above left The massive pediment that tops the fireplace and the pilasters that decorate the walls in the State Room echo the architectural ornament used on the external façade of the Mansion House. **Above right** The entrance hall leading to the main stairs is furnished with several items of local interest. A portrait of Alderman James Rowe, by the noted Yorkshire artist Henry Pickering, hangs on the wall. Next to it stands a longcase clock of 1730 by Henry Hindley of York. This timepiece, and another one in the Guildhall, earned Hindley the freedom of the city.

At the top of the stairs is the small Yellow Drawing Room with a fireplace brought from Robert Adam's Adelphi Terrace in London. Its frieze has been reset upside down. The state room is the main ceremonial chamber: it overlooks the square and embodies the pomp and autonomy of a great civic corporation. Corinthian pilasters and green and gilt panelling rise to a coved ceiling. At each end are large fireplaces topped by the coats of arms of the Crown and the City of York. Large portraits of kings and mayors are arranged such that the dignity of the one does not detract from the majesty of the other.

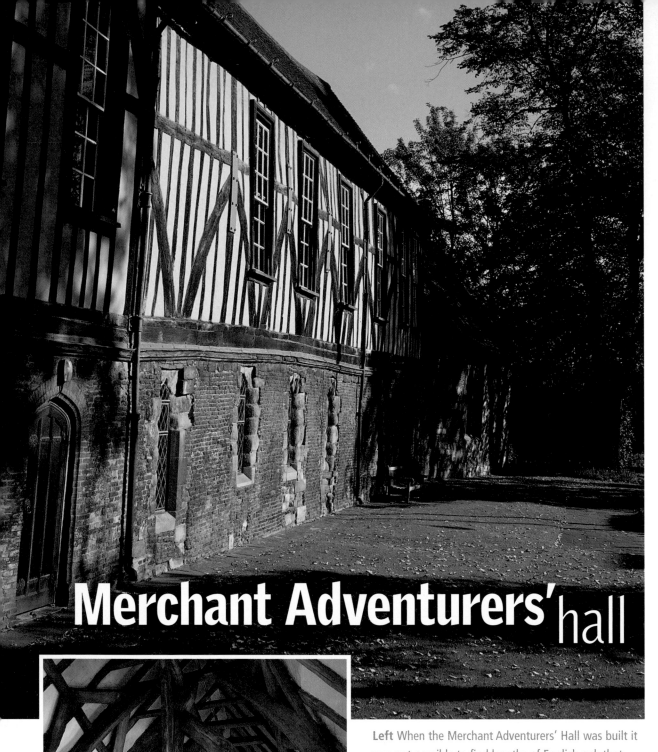

Merchant Adventurers' hall

Left When the Merchant Adventurers' Hall was built it was not possible to find lengths of English oak that could span the whole width of the structure. Therefore, the hall was constructed as a 'double nave' with two pitched roofs. Marks made on the timbers by the medieval carpenters can still be seen today. These identified the different sections of the building, made elsewhere then assembled *in situ*. **Right** On the ground floor of the hall is the undercroft. Evidence of its former inhabitants can still be seen in the scorch marks on the pillars, made by candles and torches, and in the storage niches for holding personal effects.

★ ★ ★ A complete surviving group of medieval guild hall and rooms

Fossgate, York; private house, open part year

Do not approach the building from Piccadilly, with its ugly shopping centre and naked gardens. From that angle, it looks suburban, even mock-Tudor. Approach instead from Fossgate, through a Tudor arch set beneath a coat of arms. Entry is into a 15th-century courtyard overhung by gables and old brickwork. The space is enclosed and intimate, with carved lintels and leaded windows, flagstones on the ground and antiquity in the air.

Merchant Adventurers' Hall is the finest medieval survivor in York; indeed, it claims to be the most complete group of guild buildings in Europe. The guilds were religious and charitable fraternities, many of which evolved into commercial oligopolies controlling apprenticeship and trade. They were the backbone of civil society in pre-Reformation England. In the City of London, they became liveried companies, most of their halls burned in the Great Fire. In York a number survive in their medieval form, still with domestic premises attached.

The Merchant Adventurers' Hall was dedicated to any who 'adventures his own money in overseas trade'. It consists of one great chamber dating from the mid-14th century, with two 'naves' divided by oak crown-posts. The roof is exposed, its curved trusses forming a textbook of medieval carpentry. The sash windows are Georgian insertions. The painted governor's dais came from the old Assize Court.

Beneath the hall is its most evocative relic. The posts of the undercroft are massive and distorted, as if buckling under the weight of money above. This was a hospice for the poor and infirm members, in use from 1373 until 1900. Here lived adventurers whose 'boats had not come home'. Niches in the walls were for them to keep their modest belongings. To one side is a remarkable four-sided fireplace, which must have suffused the room with heat. It gave all inmates 'a place by the fire'. The room contains a display of copies of medieval guild banners that would once have been paraded through the streets (as today in Siena).

Overlooking the courtyard is a series of Tudor service rooms, offering privacy to the Governor and his court. Three ante-rooms precede admission to the governor's presence. Today, most are filled with company memorabilia and portraits.

Middlethorpe hall

☆ ☆ Ironmaster's William-and-Mary mansion

Bishopthorpe Road, York; now a hotel

Right In the gardens, features have been arranged in imitation of an enfilade. A statue set in the centre of a pond leads the eye towards a path then on towards another garden ornament, framed in an archway.

Middlethorpe is a handsome William-and-Mary mansion standing in its own grounds opposite York Racecourse. ''Tis a very pritty place,' said Lady Mary Wortley Montagu in 1713, and it still is. The house was built for Thomas Barlow, son of a family of iron-masters, cutlers and Quakers of Sheffield and Leeds, one of many rich young men of the 18th century who began what Giles Worsley calls the 'slow drift from industry to gentry that was the characteristic of descendants of the post-Restoration ironmasters'. It has been true of the rich throughout English history.

Thomas Barlow acquired 'arms' as a knight but did not feel secure enough to set up as a gentleman near Sheffield, instead acquiring the manor of Middlethorpe in 1698. By 1702, he had built himself a new house 'in the Italian mode' and ten years later took himself and his son on a Grand Tour. When they reached France he promptly died. His son sold his manufacturing interests and invested in land.

The house remained unaltered but increasingly derelict over its life. Like many large houses, it sought a future as a school, as flats, even as Brummels Nightclub 'where the age of Regency elegance lives on'. Not until the 1980s did the York sprawl loom on the horizon and bring Middlethorpe and its proximity to the racecourse to the attention of the hotel industry. This proved its salvation. Its rescuer and owner is Historic House Hotels.

The interior has been immaculately restored, with little atmosphere of a hotel. Beyond the entrance hall with fine doorcases is the stair hall facing the garden. A bright enfilade of reception rooms runs along the garden front. The stairs have thickly carved treads and balusters and rest on a fine Corinthian column. The walls are hung with old family portraits, albeit of poor quality. To the right of the hall is a small panelled library with Piranesi prints. Beyond is the old ballroom, now the drawing room.

On the left of the hall is the Oak Room, with Ionic pilasters and panelling that breaks forward in Baroque fashion round the fireplace. Single-storey wings give the house a graceful profile to the gardens.

St William's college

⋆ ⋆ Medieval priests' college

Minster Yard, York; private house, open all year

The present buildings were erected in the 1450s as accommodation for priests at the Minster. The arrangement would have been collegiate, with staircases and rooms off them. A large hall was positioned in the north range, facing the entrance across the courtyard. The building was sold at the Dissolution and occupied by the Earl of Carlisle while he was building Castle Howard. It was reacquired by the Minster in 1902 and converted as a conference centre.

Had it not been for the heavy-handedness of the conversion by the architect, Temple Moore, medieval St William's might outshine the Merchant Adventurers' Hall. Moore refashioned the street façade in conventional neo-Tudor, with an orderly roof and shop windows along a stone-built ground floor. Inside, he rebuilt the screens passage and Great Hall as an entrance hall with, behind it, a two-storeyed structure. The upper part of this hall is now the Maclagan Hall, with some original roof timbering. The frontispiece is 17th century.

The best feature of the college is the quiet courtyard where visitors can refresh themselves after the exertions of visiting the Minster next door.

'Tis a very pritty place," said Lady Mary Wortley Montagu in 1713, and it still is.'

Treasurer's house

Above The Treasurer's House has been built over many earlier structures, including a Roman Road. In the cellar, ghostly sightings of marching centurions have been reported. However, they are visible only from the knees up, since the original road surface that they supposedly tread is some depth below the current floor. **Right** During his renovations of the house, Frank Green was responsible for creating the Great Hall. A floor that had been added in the 18th century was removed to open up the room. **Below** The West Sitting Room was another chamber re-shaped by Green. A larger room was divided to create this one, dominated by the massive fireplace, featuring a sculpture of Leda and the Swan.

Above Frank Green, the rescuer of the Treasurer's House, in a portrait by J.R.G. Exley.

 Edwardian restoration of a Jacobean house

Minster Yard, York; National Trust, open part year

Many historic buildings are museums trying to look like homes. The Treasurer's House was a home trying to look like a museum. The treasurer was that of the medieval Minster, an office of great wealth and little work, abolished at the Reformation. 'The Treasure having been confiscated, there is no further need of a Treasurer,' said a contemporary record. The house became the archbishop's residence but was then successively demolished, rebuilt, altered, sold, divided and left to decay. What we see today is the creation of one man, Frank Green, who seized the ghosts of its past and refashioned them after his own educated imagination.

Green was a scion of upwardly mobile Wakefield entrepreneurs. Fastidious, effete, unmarried and a great connoisseur, he cuts a fine figure alongside his father dressed in hunting clothes in a picture in the guidebook. He bought the Treasurer's House in 1897 and worked with Temple Moore to strip away its Victorian accretions and reinstate what he took to be the 17th-century original. Rooms were carefully designed to reproduce periods appropriate to his art and antiques. Christopher Hussey of *Country Life* was an admirer of Green, regarding his furniture as 'one of the finest collections in England'. He gave the house intact to the National Trust in 1930.

By then Green was completely eccentric. He slept each night in fresh Jaeger sheets, having them laundered in London and sent up by train. He was fanatically tidy, creeping downstairs at night to

Above The magnificent darkly panelled Dining Room at the Treasurer's House is saved from gloom by the richly moulded stucco ceiling, attributed to Cortese, and the imposing 18th-century fireplace. The cross-beams divide the ceiling's central oval into quarters, with each segment filled with decoration. The overmantel frames a Flemish landscape painting.

the kitchen to check that the cutlery lay in proper rows in the drawers. Workmen had to wear slippers indoors. Yet his attention to decorative detail, including fabric and wallpaper, created a remarkable work of Edwardian revival. Lady Diana Cooper encountered him as a girl on his antique-hunting expeditions. 'We thought him sound as a bell,' she recalled, 'until one day he admitted to veering towards Victorian taste. We stopped our ears.'

Each of the rooms seems to hang on a single work. The entrance hall has arabesque wall paintings copied from a house in King's Lynn. The West Sitting Room, fashioned from a larger room, has a voluptuous Baroque chimneypiece. The hall was entirely Green's creation, based on the conjectured location of a medieval hall. Beyond is the Blue Drawing Room, with panelling from floor to ceiling, its details picked out in bronze.

The William-and-Mary staircase is papered in green and leads to Green's sumptuous bedrooms. Each drips with canopies, drapes and panelling. The Queen's and Princess Victoria's Rooms recall a much-prized royal visit in 1900. The King's Room veers towards the absurd: a gigantic bed, reputedly from Houghton House in Norfolk, has been crammed into a simple 16th-century chamber with stencilled walls. It is like squeezing a cardinal's retinue into a Quaker meeting house.

The loveliest room is the dining room. This has an 18th-century fireplace and overmantel framing a Flemish landscape. In the plaster ceiling, a central oval incorporates what appear to be earlier cross-beams. The kitchen has been 'Trustified', but we can still imagine the old man running his finger along a shelf to check for dust and complaining of an out-of-place three-pronged fork.

York Castle museum:
the debtors' prison

☆ Surviving cells of old city prison

Tower Street, York; museum, open all year

York's Castle Museum has the finest 'historic lifestyle' display in England. It embraces the history of the North from cottage hearth and chocolate factory to fine Jacobean and Georgian interiors. There are sounds and smells as well as sights. Over it hangs a pall, that it occupies the old city jail and makes no attempt to hide the fact. Here people lived and died in misery. A graffiti notes: 'This Prison is a House of Care, a Grave for Man Alive, A Touch Stone to Try a Friend, No Place for Man to Thrive.'

The centre block was built in 1701 in the style of Vanbrugh and was for debtors. They were allowed more salubrious quarters and could work to pay off their debt. From the outside, it might be a palace were it not for the grilles on the ground floor windows and the absence of a door. Carr of York later built a wing for female prisoners and various exercise yards to the rear. Two old York streets have been reconstructed in these yards, Kirkgate and Half Moon Court.

The surviving rooms of the old jail are in the basement of the Debtors' Prison. These are the cells for those who had committed serious crimes and were awaiting sentence of death or deportation. There were 200 of these cells in the early 19th century. They are well displayed, without the ghoulishness considered obligatory in prison museums elsewhere. The condemned cell has a charcoal stove, fire and bed. It is where Dick Turpin, the celebrated highwayman, supposedly spent his last night before being hanged in 1739.

Left Dick Turpin reputedly spent his last night in this cell at York prison before he was hanged at York Tyburn on 7th April, 1739. He had fled north, a wanted man, after a career of violent robbery and even murder. He assumed the name John Palmer, but was caught horse-stealing and, after his identity was revealed, condemned to death.

South Y

Cusworth Hall

South Yorkshire

Serene marble statues stand vigil in the hall at Brodsworth. The rounded arches that spring from classical pilasters create a perfect setting for the Thellusson collection of Italian sculpture.

Brodsworth hall

✦ ✦ A Victorian mansion in grand Italianate style

At Brodsworth, 6 miles NW of Doncaster; English Heritage, open part year

The story of this house starts with a court case. The grandson of a Huguenot refugee and banker, Théophile Thellusson died in 1797 and willed that his fortune be left to accumulate during the lifetimes of all his surviving male descendants. Only when his great-grandson had died could his money pass to his sons' lineal descendants. Should none exist, it was to be used to pay off the National Debt. This was considered so unfair, and potentially destabilizing to the national economy, that it was bitterly contested. Such wills were made illegal by Act of Parliament in 1800.

By the time the inheritance fell due, in 1856, lawyers had taken most of it, but enough survived for Charles Thellusson, a yachting enthusiast with six children, to demolish and rebuild the family home at Brodsworth. The new house was inherited by each of his four sons in turn, all dying childless. It then passed to a daughter, Constance. I first visited the house in 1989 when her granddaughter, Pamela Williams, and her husband were vainly trying to keep out rain and damp while living in one room round an oil heater. It was a desperate sight. The National Trust was uninterested and she finally pleaded with English Heritage to help. The house was reopened in 1995.

Brodsworth was completed in 1863. It is long, low and Italianate, and hugely improved by stone cleaning. It looks like a mansion in London's Kensington Palace Gardens. The entrance front boasts a fine *porte-cochère*.

Two projecting bays and copious urns on a balustraded roof enliven the symmetrical garden façade. Whereas earlier country houses have a parade of reception rooms for entertaining, Brodsworth's rooms are more attuned to middle-class domesticity. This is borne out by the names of the rooms: morning room, smoking room and library. Servants are not banished to an attic but given respectable quarters behind a baize door in a wing of their own. The rooms are spacious without being extravagant. Show is confined chiefly to the hall and staircase. The architect was the little-known Philip Wilkinson, while an unknown Italian, Chevalier Casentini, contributed to the garden buildings.

The furnishings were almost all from the London firm of Lapworths and survive virtually intact: painted walls, stained glass, silk curtains and Axminster carpets. In the hall is Thellusson's collection of Italian marble sculptures, mostly sentimental Victorian works such as Pietro Magni's *Swinging Girl*. Other than a family Lawrence in the dining room and some equestrian pictures in the billiard room, the paintings are not distinguished but admirably complement the decoration. Bedrooms and lesser rooms are enjoyably furnished with the paraphernalia of the time. The fully equipped kitchen and pantries display life 'below stairs'.

The original park has been curtailed, but the formal gardens, Quarry Garden and Target Range (for archery) survive and are maintained with 1860s vigour and smartness.

Cannon hall

An early 18th-century house with interiors by Carr of York

At Cawthorne, 4 miles W of Barnsley; museum, open part year

Cannon Hall is Barnsley's lung, if not its heart. The house dominates a long, landscaped slope and is now a museum and art gallery. It was built by the local Spencer family in the 18th century on the wealth of iron. Wealth led to art and the Spencer-Stanhopes became members of the Pre-Raphaelite circle. The walls of the house display their paintings and works from the National Loans Collection Trust.

The core of the house is *c*1700 but the entrance and much of the interior were altered and decorated by Carr of York in the 1760s. This was to display Grand Tour treasures brought back by the bachelor dilettante, John Spencer. The adjacent Oak Room appears to survive from the earlier house, the panelling over its fireplace dated 1697.

The south front rooms are mostly by Carr. The dining room has an excellent Rococo ceiling depicting musical instruments. The Georgian sideboard is designed to conceal its mundane purpose of knife storage. The urns on either side of the fireplace conceal basins for washing glasses.

The library displays the taste of a provincial gentleman of the Regency era. Plasterwork depicts hunting and country pursuits. Books indicate classical taste and a love of nature. The bookcases are original, bar one which came from the old *Times* offices in Printing House Square. In the Ballroom is a large chimneypiece from Florence, decorated with the Spencer and related coats of arms. The Red Damask Room contains Spencer-Stanhope portraits, including Pre-Raphaelite works, covering seven generations of the family. This theme is repeated in photographs in the corridors.

Cannon Hall is Barnsley's lung, if not its heart.'

John Roddam Spencer-Stanhope 1829–1908

Below The ballroom at Cannon Hall is hung with the Mortlake Tapestry, a fine example of the textile arts. The large collection at the Hall includes paintings from the 17th to 20th centuries, as well as furniture, pottery and glass. The Hall is also home to the museum of the 13th/18th Royal Hussars (Queen Mary's Own) and Light Dragoons, a regiment who saw action in the Crimea and played a part in the Charge of the Light Brigade.

John Roddam Spencer-Stanhope was a second son, not destined to inherit. After an education at Oxford he became an artist and member of the Pre-Raphaelites. Among his associates were Dante Gabriel Rossetti, one of the founder members of the group, and Edward Burne-Jones.

Pre-Raphaelite artists sought a return to what they saw as the simplicity and honesty of art before Raphael. They favoured subjects with a moral meaning, often drawn from myths or religious stories. They were heavily influenced by medieval art and ideals, and this showed clearly in their choice of both subject matter and style.

Spencer-Stanhope worked with Rossetti, occupying the studio next to him at Blackfriars. It was here that he painted one of his best-known works, *Thoughts of the Past*, now in Tate Britain. A typical Pre-Raphaelite painting, it shows a young woman, a prostitute, deep in melancholy thought. The painting also shows how heavily Spencer-Stanhope was influenced by the romantic style of Burne-Jones.

Conisbrough castle

★ Norman castle with heavily buttressed round keep

At Conisbrough, 4½ miles SW of Doncaster; English Heritage, open all year

Forget dreary South Yorkshire for a moment and concentrate on Conisbrough keep on its hill overlooking the River Don. 'In the beauty of its geometrical simplicity,' wrote Pevsner, it is 'unsurpassed in England'. The keep survives almost intact, a monument to medieval might. It inspired Walter Scott's castle of the Saxon kings in *Ivanhoe*, drawing Victorian tourists *en masse*, and is still managed by the Ivanhoe Trust on behalf of English Heritage.

Conisbrough is pure Norman. It was built in *c*1180 apparently to his own design by Hamelin Plantagenet, son of Geoffrey of Anjou. The plan is found elsewhere only in Plantagenet's castle at Mortemer in Normandy. The form is of a single round keep on a large mound, with clinging buttresses battered outwards at their bases to resist sapping.

The first-floor entrance is reached along a causeway, lethally exposed from above. The lower storeys can be reached only by a ladder. There are no windows on the first floor, which was for storage. The lord's chamber was on the second floor, later supplanted by a Great Hall located elsewhere in the surrounding, mostly vanished, bailey.

This room has a large fireplace with a giant hood. Above is the solar with a small chapel contained within one of the buttresses. The keep retains its staircases, garderobes and alcoves, remarkable in a building of this age. It is otherwise empty.

The interiors are displayed for primary school children. On the ground floor a tape recording recites over and again that 'the walls of the castle have ears'. From the roof is a view over the few remaining trees of the Don Valley.

Left The size of the fireplace that remains on the second floor of the keep at Conisbrough is a clear indication of the importance of the original room. It was the chamber of the Lord of the Castle, where he would have conducted his daily business before retreating to the privacy of the solar on the floor above. The keep was designed to be impregnable and water tanks and a bread oven at the top of the tower ensured the self-sufficiency of the community at time of siege. A roof and floors have now been reinstated.

DONCASTER
Cusworth hall

✶ ✶ Merchant's house with plasterwork by Joseph Rose

2 miles W of Doncaster; museum and grounds, open all year
(due to restoration work the house is closed until end 2006; the grounds remain open)

The house was built for William Wrightson in 1740 in fine parkland on a hill overlooking Doncaster. The architect was a local man, George Platt, but the ubiquitous James Paine (also working on the town's Mansion House) soon took over. The entrance forecourt displays a comfortable Georgian mansion in crumbling stone, enclosed by service wings. The garden front looks out over the Don Valley, which must once have been a splendid view. The house is owned by the local council and is desperately in need of full restoration. A fine house is struggling to get out.

Few rooms are free of museumitis, yet behind the stands and display cases can be detected fine plasterwork by Adam's stuccoist, Joseph Rose. The small library is a delight, with Gothick bookcases set into the walls. It is the only instance I know of bookshelves continuing low over a fireplace, with no care for the fate of the precious leather.

Cusworth's treasure is its chapel, again with plasterwork by Rose. It might be the private oratory of a Roman cardinal, which may have been Wrightson's intention. There is a classical screen to the apse and the walls are being stripped to reveal religious murals that appear to fill the room, some by Francis Hayman. These are now being restored.

Mansion house

Above From the entrance hall, the main staircase rises to a dramatic landing where it halts and divides in two before carrying on up to the first floor. Two Italian statues of pageboys bearing lamps stand guard.

★★ Georgian townhouse by James Paine with grand ballroom

High Street, Doncaster; civic building, open by arrangement only

Doncaster Mansion House is one of only three in England of this splendour (with York and City of London). It was commissioned from James Paine in 1744 and stands prominent on a bend in the High Street. It is like a Georgian buck lost in a suburban supermarket. How much civic pride Doncaster must once have boasted, and how little it displays today, a place of ring roads and cheap stores.

The house is a brash townhouse of three grand bays, designed when Paine was working on Cusworth Hall. The façade has a rusticated ground floor, attached columns and three large windows to the first-floor ballroom. The doorway is deeply recessed, as if welcoming visitors into a masonic temple. The entrance hall is all red carpet and green scagliola. The stair rises dramatically to a Venetian window, doubling back on itself, its handrail adorned with acanthus balusters.

The ballroom is magnificent for what was then a small town. A punctilious official told me that it cost £4,523.4s.6d when built. Joseph Rose was commissioned to do the Rococo plasterwork. It has been repainted fiercely by Crown Paints, apparently true to the original colours. Doors and doorcases, inside and outside the ballroom, are beautifully made. To each side, again through fine doors, are the mayoress's withdrawing room and the grand saloon. Would that civic pride in England might one day be permitted to repeat such glory elsewhere.

DONCASTER

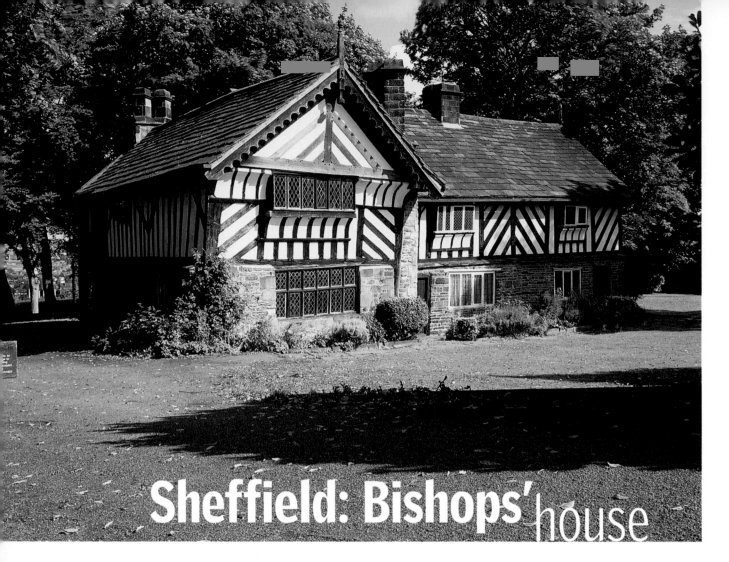

Sheffield: Bishops' house

★ Medieval farmhouse surviving in a suburban park

At Norton, 2 miles S of Sheffield; museum, open all year

Sheffield has little of architectural note. Nowhere has been so harshly treated by de-industrialization and has so little to show for its 20th-century urban renewal. Bishops' House is the best bet in a small park, Meersbrook, in the village of Norton on the southern outskirts of the city.

The house is a timber-framed structure, hardly large enough to be considered manorial. It dates from the 15th century when it was a farmhouse owned by the Blythe family, ancestors of a Bishop Blythe after whose job it is named. A council parks employee lived here until it was restored as a museum.

The exterior is jolly enough, with black-and-white timbering above a rough stone ground floor. Most of the windows look original, with some projecting oriels. The plan is L-shaped, with a central hall and parlour and upstairs chambers in the cross-wing. Although the core of the house is Tudor, the domestic wing was extended in the 17th century.

The former Great Parlour is laid out as a dining room with period furniture and pewter. The Hall is bare, with some revealed fragments of ornamental panelling. Upstairs is more interesting. There are two crude but attractive plaster overmantels, one with fruit trees growing inside Renaissance arches, the other with two ferocious dogs and a winged head of a man. These date from the mid-17th century when William Blythe was a Parliamentary army officer. The vast floorboards are only half dressed, their bark still showing in the cracks.

Wentworth castle

⋆ ⋆   Magnificent façade of northern Baroque palace

3½ miles SW of Barnsley; private house, now a college; gardens open by arrangement

The castle is a palatial house built in 1670 and extended by the Wentworths in the 18th century. It is now a college. Most of the rooms have been institutionalized and their fireplaces removed, sold and dispersed, but the fine gardens are accessible and discreet glimpses may be had of the interior by appointment. The three main façades are magnificent.

The original house is the modest seven-bay front facing north towards the entrance drive. There is a scrolly pediment over the main porch and a Restoration staircase inside, rightly described by Pevsner as 'thickly and juicily carved'. Round the corner to the left and overlooking the valley to the east is an architectural trumpet blast. This façade was erected c1710–20 by Thomas Wentworth, later Earl of Strafford. He should not be confused with his earlier namesake at neighbouring Wentworth Woodhouse, which this house was meant to rival. Our Wentworth, Lord Raby at the time, was ambassador in Berlin and returned with a design by Jean de Bodt, architect of the Arsenal at Potsdam, for a house in the Franco-Prussian manner. Lord Montagu had likewise built at Boughton (Northamptonshire).

The façade is of extraordinary grandeur, a far cry from the timid Yorkshire Baroque of, for instance, Newby or Beningbrough. Two storeys of black-ochre stone rise to an attic buried beneath a parapet. The windows are elaborately

'The grounds
of Wentworth Castle
are of Burlingtonian
stateliness.'

Left Work began on Stainborough Castle in 1727. It is built on the site of an iron-age hill fort and occupies the highest point on the estate at Wentworth, 600ft (200m) above sea level. It was intended to be the culmination of a tour of the grounds.
Right The ionic Rotunda was also originally meant to be a focal point in the garden, and once stood on a grassy hill, clear of vegetation. It was started in 1742 by Thomas Wentworth's son, William, and is modelled on the temple of Hercules at Tivoli, outside Rome.

pedimented. The centre has three big arched windows on the first floor. These are divided by pilasters and crowned with a mass of foliage and heraldry. The composition is unmistakably by a continental.

Nor is this all. The far frontage onto the garden is later, of the early 1760s and in a purer Palladian style. It is of rusticated stone, with a central portico, and with Venetian windows in the end pavilions. Inside, the grand east range has a first-floor long gallery of stupendous proportions, apparently completed by James Gibbs. It is closed to public view, perhaps to conceal its misuse. That a building should be so treated in the cause of education is wrong.

The grounds of Wentworth Castle are of Burlingtonian stateliness. They include a folly castle (Stainborough Castle), an obelisk, a rotunda and the customary temples. Beside the entrance from the main road is an open-sided market cross. The last stands on 16 columns with drum bases like a Roman temple, sadly purposeless. It was allegedly designed by Horace Walpole, presumably as an antiquarian folly.

Wentworth Woodhouse

⭐ Façade of great house in park

At Wentworth, 5 miles NW of Rotherham; private house and grounds, east front visible from public right-of-way

Wentworth is one of the most splendid houses-in-a-landscape in England. It claims the longest continuous façade in the country, of 600ft. Its closure to public access behind security fences is a crying shame. John Carr's massive stables are locked, occupied on my visit by mangy pheasants pecking at barbed wire. Behind more wire is an encampment of Georgian outhouses and a derelict 1960s teacher training college. I include the house because its exterior is fully visible from the TransPennine Way, passing directly in front, and in the hope of better things to come. Even today, Wentworth Woodhouse cuts a dash in an oasis between the outskirts of Sheffield, Rotherham and Barnsley.

The original house was built by Thomas Wentworth, 1st Earl of Strafford, in the 1630s.

'Wentworth Woodhouse **ranked with Harewood** and **Castle Howard** among the **great mansions** of the North.'

He was executed by the Parliamentarians in 1641. This house was transformed in the 1720s by another Thomas Wentworth, later Marquis of Rockingham, in the Baroque style. Fluted pilasters flank decorated windows with a giant cartouche overhead.

In 1734, with this transformation just complete, plans for a completely new east range, back-to-back with the old, were shown to Lord Burlington's Committee of Taste by Henry 'Burlington Harry' Flitcroft. The design was similar to Colen Campbell's vanished Wanstead but grander by far. This was to be the biggest house in England and probably still is. The front is nineteen bays long, with a double flight of steps in the middle, rising to an entrance portico. Wings seem to flow without ceasing from either side, each section a house in itself. These wings end in corner pavilions with cupolas added by Carr of York in the 1780s.

Behind this front are rooms designed by Flitcroft and filled by Rockingham and his successors over the years with an epic collection of art. Wentworth Woodhouse ranked with Harewood and Castle Howard among the great mansions of the North. When Arthur Mee visited it in the 1940s, he saw it as 'standing astonishing witness to the commonplace grandeur of the 18th century'.

The house displayed portraits of kings, queens, Straffords and Rockinghams by van Dyck, Lely and Reynolds. There was a painting by Stubbs of the celebrated horse, *Whistlejacket*, and Hogarth's Rockingham family group. Even the austere Pevsner called this a house of 'quite exceptional value ... from the Viennese or Venetian gaiety ... to the Palladian purity ... not easily matched anywhere in England'.

The house is no longer the property of the Fitzwilliam-Wentworth Estate, may God rest its soul. The contents are dispersed, although some are retained by the family elsewhere. The building belongs to a retired architect from London who, I am told, means well.

West Y

Harewood House

West Yorkshire

Bradford: Bolling hall

Right Among the many treasures on display at Bolling Hall is this magnificent couch bed by Thomas Chippendale, topped with gilded decoration and hung with rich red damask. A selection of the paintings owned by the City of Bradford can also be seen at the museum. **Below** Bolling Hall has been added to at several times during its history. The oldest segment of the building is the pele tower, far left in the picture, which now forms the entrance to the hall.

✩✩ Jacobean house built round a pele tower, with additions by Carr of York

Bowling Hall Road, Bradford; museum, open all year

Right The Ghost Room is reputed to be the scene of a 17th-century haunting. The Royalist Earl of Newcastle was staying here while his army besieged Parliamentarian Bradford, and one day he vowed to kill every inhabitant. That night a ghost appeared at his bedside, crying 'Pity poor Bradford'. Much shaken, the Earl ordered a more moderate attack and only ten lives were lost.

Black the landscape, black the Hall and, on a rainy March day, black the effort of trying to find this dignified old Yorkshire lady in the suburbs of Bradford. Bolling Hall looks indestructible.

The house was founded by the Bollings in the Middle Ages, from which survives a large pele tower. This is a formidable thing to find in deeply urban Yorkshire. It passed to the Tempests of Broughton, who added a hall to the tower, and then to Saviles, Lindleys and Woods. The last employed Carr of York in 1779 to redesign the east wing. Surrounded by mineral workings, the house declined until taken over by the council in 1912. From the garden to the south, there is a magnificent view of the pele, Hall, Georgian wing and balancing tower.

The entrance is under the pele tower, with an impressive medieval kitchen. The hall, known in these parts as the housebody, was altered internally in the 18th century, with an unusual balcony linking the tower to the east wing. The massive window contains 17th-century heraldic glass depicting the Bolling and Tempest families. Carr's rooms in the east wing, ornate and rather cold, are used to display Bradford's admirable collection of 18th-century furniture.

Upstairs are two Carr rooms. One contains a great treasure, a Chippendale couch bed in red damask made for Harewood House (see page 164) and acquired by Bradford in 1976, much to its credit. At the back is a room dedicated to a famous son of Bradford, Frederick Delius. It includes his piano and Yorkshire furniture in the Art Nouveau style. Beyond the Hall is the Ghost Room, alive with wood carving and a geometrical plaster frieze. The pele tower contains a mid-1400s chamber with painted hangings in place of tapestries, a rarity.

Bramham park

★★ Queen Anne mansion with grounds created on Baroque principles

At Bramham, 6 miles S of Wetherby; private house and garden, house open by appointment only, gardens open part year

Bramham is a rare example of Baroque landscape principles applied to a domestic English house. The languid approach from the main road gradually forms into a magnificent composition of courtyard, house and grounds. On all sides are the intersecting vistas beloved of the early Georgians aping Le Notre (influential designer of the park at Versailles), and detested by the later ones. Somehow these formal ponds, cascades, obelisks and temples survived the clean sweep of Capability Brown and the Romantics elsewhere.

The house was built *c*1705–10 by Robert Benson, Lord Bingley, in a style that barely hints at Baroque. The main block is flanked by service wings round a central courtyard rising up the slope. Only the curving coach ramp and steps to the front door yield much sense of theatre. The central doorway misses a grander storey above. The steps to the garden entrance behind are more successful, a scene of swaying architectural motion.

Bramham was mostly gutted in a fire of 1828 and left derelict for eighty years. In 1906, a Bingley descendant, George Richard Lane Fox, commissioned Detmar Blow to restore the old house. Blow left battered stone walls in the entrance hall, as savaged by the fire, a picturesque touch. Richness is confined to the 17th-century chandelier and huge pictures by Kneller and Reynolds. The Long Gallery is neo-Queen Anne, hung with family portraits. Centrepiece of the room is a Louis XV bureau with beautiful swirling inlay.

The appointments system is eccentric. I was refused pre-arranged admission as the hall was in use for yoga.

Left Dominating the Long Gallery is the *dos-a-dos* bureau, believed to have been made for Louis XV of France. This is, effectively, a double, or 'back-to-back' desk. Both sides of the bureau open out to provide a workspace for two people.
Below The Hall is a perfect cube in shape, and still bears marks from the fire of 1828. For 80 years it was covered only by a temporary roof, then the rebuilt house roof served as the ceiling until 1990 when restoration of the Hall was completed. The Long Gallery and the bureau can be seen through the double doors.

Gomersall: Oakwell hall

✫ ✫ Elizabethan house with painted panelling and literary connections

At Birstall, 1 mile NW of Gomersal; museum, open all year

Charlotte Brontë used Elizabethan Oakwell as the model for Fieldhead in *Shirley*. She called it, 'neither grand nor comfortable; within as without it was antique, rambling and incommodious'. An Edwardian tenant was a Batley lawyer, George Maggs, who forestalled a plan to ship the hall to America, where such buildings are more valued. In 1928, it was handed instead to the local council.

So many Yorkshire yeomen's houses have vanished that the survival of any one is a miracle. Oakwell sits back from the road, with space enough to distance itself from the Batley to Bradford sprawl. The core of the house is late 16th century but the fine panelling, ceilings and fireplaces are 17th.

The house's first remarkable feature is its façade. Close-mullioned windows fill the entire front wall of the Hall, with wide sweeping gables on the wings on either side. Inside, the Hall has original Doric columns to its screen and the stairs have openwork dog-gates. The Great Parlour is richly decorated, with crude caryatids flanking the window bays and panelling painted in *trompe-l'œil*, known as scumbling. Most of the designs are abstract, but over the mantelpiece they include delightful landscapes.

The Great Parlour Chamber above has a large Elizabethan bed and a garderobe. The remaining rooms have been appropriately furnished, many with old chests. A bed exhorts its occupant to 'Drede God, Love God, Prayes God'. The Painted Chamber to the rear of the house has similar scumbling to the Parlour downstairs, grained to look like walnut. This is a great rarity since most oak panelling was later stripped to reveal its grain, a habit recently extended to pine. The bed in the New Parlour Chamber has massive turned posts on square plinths, like thick Jacobean calves stuck in monstrous shoes.

In the roof space above the kitchen is a rare Kitchen Chamber. Here food would hang and servants sleep, warmed from the fires below.

Below In the Hall at Oakwell, dogs were kept in their place by a set of gates at the foot of the stairs. The gates are heavily pierced and carved in a pattern that complements the decoration of the banisters. **Below right** The wood lining the walls of the Great Parlour is painted to mimic a more ornate style of panelling, using a now rarely seen technique known as scumbling. In *Shirley*, Charlotte Brontë described the parlour as 'Very mellow in colouring and tasteful in effect ...'.

Gomersall: Red house

⭐ Georgian cloth merchant's house and inspiration for Charlotte Brontë

Oxford Road, Gomersal; museum, open all year

This is a cloth merchant's house of the 'middling' sort. It was built by and for the Taylor family in the 1660s and owned by them until 1920. In the 1830s, one of Joshua Taylor's six children, Mary, became a close friend of Charlotte Brontë from Haworth. Brontë featured the family and house in her novel, *Shirley*, as she did Oakwell Hall (see page 158). It is from this association that the building draws much of its celebrity.

The house sits by the main road, and is called Red for the unusual colour of its brick construction. The outside is Georgian, as is much of the interior, although the latter suffers severely from museumitis. The rooms are all pretty-genteel. The Hall is painted to look like stone, the pine wood grained to resemble mahogany and the arches 'marbled'. Stained-glass heads of Milton and Shakespeare adorn the dining room. It is as described by Brontë, 'no splendour but taste everywhere'.

Waxwork figures portray the Taylors at work and play. The women paint watercolours, the children are tutored. Other tableaux in the house show the servants in the kitchens, well equipped with original implements.

Below The Red House became Briarmains in Charlotte Brontë's novel *Shirley*. Among the features of the house that she describes in the book are the stained-glass windows in the dining room which show '... the suave head of William Shakespeare, and the serene one of John Milton', each depicted in a 'gravely tinted medallion'.

HALIFAX Holdsworth house

★ Jacobean house with unusual windows

2 miles N of Halifax; now a hotel

The setting of Holdsworth House must once have been sublime, in its private cleft in the moors. It now stands in a grimy valley, full of the scars and shedlands north of Halifax. But the exterior is a fine display of Yorkshire Jacobean, built *c*1598 and extended in the early 17th century. The porch is dated 1633. The formal entrance is through noble gateposts into a knot garden. An original gazebo is in one corner and muscular stone walls flank the sides.

The main façade is extraordinary, crowded with thick-mullioned windows. This is well-set, virile Yorkshire. The porch has to its right two gabled bays, one with a cross of St John indicating past Crusader activity on someone's part. The lower hall window has eleven lights, asymmetrically arranged. The left wing has a two-tier window composition, again with a wide gable. It is all most assertive. Older byres and barns extend behind.

The interior is much altered but contains Jacobean furnishings, beams and fireplaces. The house was acquired by the Pearson family in 1963 and turned into a country club for dining and gambling. In 1964 it achieved immortality as the venue for John Lennon's twenty-fourth birthday party. Guests can still sleep in beds in which the Beatles are alleged to have slept that night, forced to sleep two to a room. The hotel literature boasts also that 'Jayne Mansfield and Sir Alec Douglas-Home slept here'. The mind boggles.

HALIFAX
Shibden hall

★★★ Medieval hall house restored in the 19th century

Lister's Road, Halifax; museum, open all year

The doyenne of Shibden was Anne Lister (1791–1840), a lesbian who left a coded journal detailing every aspect of a propertied lady's life in late-Georgian Yorkshire. Many entries run to 2000 words a day. It was Anne who restored the house in Jacobethan style in the 1830s. She reopened the Hall to the roof and installed new beams and a neo-Gothic tower.

Shibden today is a superb medieval hall house, periodically updated but with its character intact. It sits on a lonely hill outside Halifax, amid a pleasant garden but surrounded by a desecrated landscape. It was built in the mid-15th century and bought in 1612 by the coal-rich Listers, who handed it to Halifax Council in 1933.

While the exterior is of blackened sandstone, the inside is a glorious mass of dark oak. The entrance is into a screens passage, off which a study takes the place of the old buttery. This has been recreated as a den of walnut furniture, leather books, old guns and smoking equipment. It lacks only smells. The Hall, a Yorkshire housebody, is lit by a twenty-light Elizabethan window, filled with family heraldry. A portrait of Anne Lister peers down from the walls. In the middle of the Hall is a fine 1590s dining table.

Beyond the Hall is the Savile drawing room, with an early English piano made by Pohlmann in 1769. The staircase, with a view from the gallery into the Hall below, was installed by Anne as part of her restoration. The Red Room is so-called for the Tudor frieze and contains a chunky four-poster with canopy. The guidebook claims that the purpose of the canopy was to protect the sleeper from falling spiders and bird droppings, which is new to me. An early powder closet guards the entrance to the Victorian library tower.

Other rooms include the tiny bedchamber in which Anne herself slept, constantly complaining to the staff that it was either too hot or too cold.

Left The kitchen at Shibden Hall has been filled with the utensils and tableware of yesteryear; the aim is to give the visitor an idea of how food was cooked in days gone by. Bowls of raw ingredients await preparation on top of the well-scrubbed kitchen table. A veritable *batterie de cuisine* hangs at the ready. A huge fireplace occupies one wall, equipped with a clockwork-driven spit on which meat would have been turned.

Harewood house

★★★★☆ A palace built by John Carr of York and Robert Adam, altered by Charles Barry

At Harewood, 8 miles N of Leeds; private house and grounds, open part year

Harewood is a place of dazzlement, a St Petersburg palace on a Yorkshire ridge. It affirms 18th-century taste, 19th-century wealth and 20th-century ingenuity, privately owned and superbly presented.

Edwin Lascelles inherited the estate which his father acquired in 1738 and, on the advice of Lord Leicester of Holkham, commissioned John Carr of York to design him a new mansion. At the same time, he turned to the thirty-three-year-old Robert Adam in 1758 for the interiors, although work on them did not begin until 1765. While the exterior was mostly Carr, the interiors were to be Adam's biggest single commission, albeit one wracked by arguments over cost and delay. Lascelles was not an easy man. Adam brought to the task his preferred team of Joseph Rose and William Collins for the plasterwork, Angelica Kauffmann, Antonio Zucchi and Biagio Rebecca for the decorative paintings. Furniture was to

'Harewood is a place of dazzlement, a St Petersburg palace on a Yorkshire ridge.'

Above When Harewood House was first built the South front looked out onto a grass field. Between 1844 and 1848 this area was transformed into an Italianate Terrace and Parterre based on plans by Sir Charles Barry. Photographs dating from as early as the 1860s show the gardens much as they appear today. The fountain at the centre of the parterre features a statue of Orpheus with a Leopard; this is a modern piece, created to replace the Victorian original that was smashed by a hard frost in the 1980s.

be exclusively by Chippendale and landscaping by Capability Brown. Harewood is a monument to them all.

Only a Victorian would have dared tamper with such work. But such was Lady Louisa Harewood, who summoned Sir Charles Barry in 1843 to add new attics and upset the delicate balance of Carr's exterior. Barry italianized the terrace façade to the rear and tampered with at least three of Adam's glorious rooms.

Harewood could take it. Entry is direct into Adam's Hall, its pillars and frieze recently painted in a colour rare in classical architecture, chocolate. In the middle is an acquisition by the present Lord Harewood, a giant Epstein of Adam. The statue was rescued from a Blackpool fun fair, to which 20th-century ridicule had consigned it. This primitive figure gazing up at his namesake's delicate ceiling might depict Beauty and the Beast. Gestures such as this, a rhythm of old and new throughout the house, give Harewood its character.

Adam's main reception rooms are charmingly interspersed with small galleries. The Old Library has one of his most serene ceilings, divided geometrically into panels filled with anthemion and other motifs, in greens and blues. Blank arches are filled with paintings or plasterwork of mythical scenes. Smaller rooms follow, including an apsidal chamber decorated by Sir Herbert Baker in 'Adam Revival' style. Closets have been converted into galleries for watercolours and modern art. Here are 20th-century works from Munnings to Piper.

Grandeur returns with Princess Mary's Sitting Room. The ceilings are now a bolder Adam, with fans containing classical plaster reliefs. The room's three Adam-Chippendale

Left The monumental alabaster figure of Adam was sculpted by Sir Jacob Epstein in 1939. It stands at the centre of Robert Adam's entrance hall. Victorian photographs show the hall filled with furniture, but today it has been restored to its former glory as a magnificent classical ante-chamber.

masterpieces, a secretaire and two commodes, were to Sacheverell Sitwell 'among the greatest work of English craftsmanship' (although he said there was a better one at Renishaw Hall, in Derbyshire). Their decorative reliefs are of exquisite inlay.

The Spanish Library displays the heavier hand of Barry. Solid bookcases now contrast with a lighthearted ceiling. In the New Library, really a saloon, we are back to Adam, the ceiling rising above a glorious coving of urn motifs dancing the length of the room.

Two further reception rooms, the Yellow and Cinnamon Drawing Rooms, show Adam at his most inventive. His ability to get teams of craftsmen to execute meticulous designs, while other clients were baying at his door, was astonishing. The Yellow Drawing Room has a Reynolds reflected in a Chippendale Rococo mirror and Chippendale furniture. The ceiling pattern is matched in the carpet. The Cinnamon Room contains portraits by Reynolds and Gainsborough.

The climax is yet to come. The Gallery at Harewood has an Adam ceiling but the walls and windows are by Barry. The walls are hung with one of the best private art collections in England. Old Masters by Bellini, Cima, Titian, Veronese and El Greco share pride of place with the view over the terrace to Capability Brown's landscape beyond.

The dining room and music room bring us back to the Hall. Almost as an afterthought, Adam leaves us with his music room, to some the most serene chamber in the house. Walls, ceiling and carpet all act as a frame for Sir Joshua Reynolds' masterpiece, *Mrs Hale and her Children*.

Right The Gallery was much altered by Charles Barry in the mid-19th century, but fortunately the original ceiling remains. Designed by Adam in 1769, its plasterwork is by Joseph Rose, with painted panels by Biagio Rebecca. Among the works on view in the Gallery are a *Madonna and Child* by Bellini and an *Allegory* by El Greco.

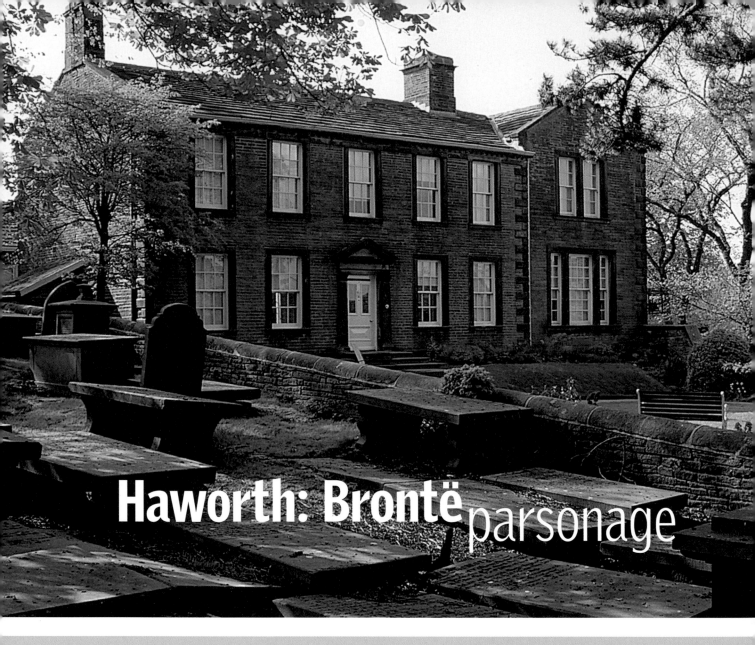

Haworth: Brontë parsonage

The Brontës

Charlotte (1816–55), Emily (1818–48) and Anne (1820–49) were the daughters of an Anglo-Irish clergyman, Patrick Brontë. Born at Thornton, near Bradford, they had two older sisters, Maria and Elizabeth, who died as children in 1825, and a brother, Branwell, who painted this famous portrait of the three writing sisters.

Despite their short lives, the Brontës were to write some of the greatest English novels. They worked together from an early age and in 1846 had a collection of their poems printed under assumed names: Charlotte, Emily and Anne Brontë became Currer, Ellis and Acton Bell respectively. The following year, Charlotte's *Jane Eyre*, Emily's *Wuthering Heights* and Anne's *Agnes Grey* all found publishers. Anne published one more novel, *The Tenant of Wildfell Hall* (1848), and Charlotte two, *Shirley* (1849) and *Villette* (1853).

Above The Brontë sisters often wrote together, this dining-room table serving as their communal desk. In the same room is the sofa on which Emily died from tuberculosis on 19th December, 1848, less than three months after the death of her brother Branwell. By May the following year Anne, too, had died, leaving Charlotte alone. Their father survived them all.

☆ Shrine to the writing sisters on the moor's edge

Church Street, Haworth, 3 miles S of Keighley; museum, open all year

England's most famous parsonage is now a shrine to the Brontë sisters, climax of the 'Haworth Experience'. The setting is remarkable. A village clings to the steep hillside outside Keighley. The shops are almost all dedicated to souvenirs. Visitors troop in their thousands up the hill towards the church. Some at least push further into the parsonage that inspired so much literary output.

Patrick Brontë came to Haworth in 1820 with his wife and six children. Two died in 1825, as did his wife in 1821; Brontë outlived them all. Even before Charlotte, Emily and Anne had died, they were famous and Haworth was a place of pilgrimage. It is to this period, the 1850s, that the Brontë Society has restored the parsonage rooms.

The survival of the environs of the house is miraculous, with churchyard in front and open moor behind. On all but the sunniest of days this can seem a sombre spot. The interiors are those of a modest house of the late 18th century, with Georgian furniture and delicate fabrics and prints. Only in the dining room, where the girls did most of their writing, can we sense the industry of the place. The room contains the sofa on which Emily died.

Upstairs is all shrine. On the landing is a copy of the brother, Branwell Brontë's, celebrated portrait of the three girls. Patrick's bedroom is as he left it. Charlotte's own room is crowded with display cases, including one containing her tiny shoes. It is worthy, but does not come alive.

Huddersfield: Longley old hall

⋆ ⋆   Much-restored Jacobean house with earlier medieval house revealed inside

At Longley, 1½ miles SE of Huddersfield; private house, open by arrangement

Longley is hidden away from central Huddersfield, through a characterless housing estate and down a cul-de-sac behind a row of cottages. A stone gable comes into view. The scene is unprepossessing. Yet the house has recently proved an architectural goldmine.

The Old Hall was owned by a prominent Huddersfield family, the Ramsdens, who in 1976 sold what they thought was a Jacobean house which had been much restored in 1884. The buyers were Robin and Christine Gallagher. Only when the Gallaghers started to remove partitions and wallpaper did they discover a medieval H-plan house within. House detectives have not left them alone ever since.

The earlier house is now immediately apparent on entering, a traditional design of two wings with linking hall, possibly dating from the 15th century. The hall was extended outwards

Above Renovations at Longley Old Hall have revealed many secrets. Work in the downstair's lavatory uncovered this early lintel, which archaeologists have dated to between 1380 and 1410. The decorative shaping visible on the bottom of the beam is called an ogee.

Right The timbers laid bare above the stairs would once have been part of an outside wall. An open door leads to a room sympathetically furnished in a 17th-century style.

in the 17th century to form a flat façade with prominent gables. The carpenters clearly had trouble with this extension since beams, trusses, cantilevers and floor levels dart off in strange directions, adding greatly to the confusion and character of the place. Portions of woodwork have been ring-dated to the 14th century. Mrs Gallagher opens cupboard doors and peels back partitions to reveal timbers of ever more puzzling significance.

The ground floor rooms have been admirably furnished in a 17th-century style, given that this is a family home. Timbers are revealed wherever panelling is absent. Upstairs was an old wool-working area, now restored. Wool bobbins were found under floorboards, some of which are so rough-hewn as to retain their bark. Old oak is said to be stronger than steel. So should be the nerves of a historic house owner.

Cliffe castle

★ Mill-owning family's Victorian mansion with Parisian-style decoration

Spring Gardens Lane, Keighley; museum, open by arrangement

Everything about Cliffe Castle suggests a J. B. Priestley novel. A Keighley family named Butterfield owned three woollen mills and grew rich. Their younger son was sent to run the export side in America. He chucked the job and in 1854 married a rich American girl, Mary Roosevelt Burke. They went to live in Paris and consorted with 'the French Imperial Court' (says the guidebook).

Butterfield then inherited the family home and, in the 1880s, decided to blow his fortune redecorating it in Parisian style. Two local architects were duly hired to re-case the entrance, hall, staircase and main reception rooms, and add towers and conservatories. These were upholstered and painted by French craftsmen.

Butterfield's son inherited Cliffe in 1910, appalled at his flamboyant father's extravagance. He stayed at home, became Mayor of Keighley, was knighted and spent nothing on the house. His daughter appears to have reverted to type. She married a Pierrepont and became Countess Manvers. She moved to Thoresby (Nottinghamshire), where her grandfather would have felt thoroughly at home, taking with her Cliffe's best contents. Disaster was only averted thanks to another local tycoon, Sir Bracewell Smith, one-time Lord Mayor of London, who stepped forward in 1950 and saved the house as a museum.

Cliffe Castle is in 'outrageous' High Victorian taste. A *porte-cochère* leads into the Hall and grand staircase. Butterfield arms, such as they are, occur everywhere. There is Powell glass in the stair window and fine Gothic arches throughout the public spaces.

Although the rest of Cliffe is now a natural history museum, the three main Butterfield rooms are in sumptuous condition, spread out through open interconnecting doors. This is Paris come to Keighley. Lush drapes hang from walls, arches and windows. Portraits of Napoleon III and the Empress Eugénie dominate the far room; these are by a court painter delightfully named Boutibonne. Cliffe is well done, a ghost of Yorkshire's finest age.

Inset (right) Butterfield certainly made his mark on Keighley when he commissioned his 'castle'. He also made sure it was stamped on Cliffe itself; reminders of the Butterfield name can be found around the house, like this capital letter B incorporated into a piece of stained glass.

Left The very picture of a wealthy Victorian textile magnate, Sir Henry Isaac Butterfield stares out in portrait and bust form over the home that he created. The original house was built in the late 1820s and was bought by the Butterfield family in 1848, when it was called Cliffe Hall. Sir Henry inherited the house in 1874, renaming it Cliffe Castle a few years later.

Below Sir Henry redecorated Cliffe in opulent style and the main reception rooms are packed with pieces that reflect his eclectic taste. Heavily patterned carpets cover the floors and compete with the different designs of wallpapers and other furnishings. There are chairs everywhere; some sit at the sides of the rooms, others are arranged around tables. Ostentatious ornaments stand on cabinets and plinths.

KEIGHLEY
East Riddlesden hall

✫ ✫ ✫ Jacobean weaving magnate's house

At Riddlesden, 1 mile NE of Keighley; National Trust, open part year

Just where the Aire Valley is at its most depressing, the scene is saved by the Murgatroyds of Riddlesden. In the 1640s, this weaving family built a handsome, now black, gritstone hall with domestic wing. Their relations, the Starkies, added another wing in 1692. The house became a farm and went downhill for two and a half centuries until acquired by the National Trust in 1934. The building sits across a wide lawn with ponds, the gabled roofline dramatic against the distant hills. Though Jacobean in date, Riddlesden is old-fashioned, essentially Elizabethan. It carries the motto 'Vive Le Roy', the Murgatroyds being staunch Royalists. The right-hand Starkie wing is clearly later and has pedimented windows on a *piano nobile*. But it was demolished behind the façade in 1905 and looks tragic. It should surely be rebuilt as someone's house.

Right The building history of East Riddlesden is hard to pin down. There was a house on the site before James Murgatroyd began his work in the 1640s and the main Hall may well have been a remnant of an earlier structure. Murgatroyd seems to have had grand plans for the room; the small fireplace set in the wall above the great fireplace is an indication that an additional floor was considered at some point.

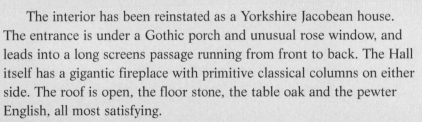

The interior has been reinstated as a Yorkshire Jacobean house. The entrance is under a Gothic porch and unusual rose window, and leads into a long screens passage running from front to back. The Hall itself has a gigantic fireplace with primitive classical columns on either side. The roof is open, the floor stone, the table oak and the pewter English, all most satisfying.

Upstairs is a corridor above the screens passage leading to two main chambers with closets. The Stairhead Chamber is rush-matted, panelled and furnished. The Grey Lady's Chamber takes its name from an occupant who was caught *in flagrante* with a lover by her husband. He locked the door and starved them to death. Or so it is said.

Downstairs, the two principal rooms, the drawing room and dining room, have elaborate plaster ceilings similar in design. Tables are carpeted and dressers piled with pewter.

Leeds: Kirkstall abbey

⭐ Substantial fragments of a Cistercian monastery

Abbey Walk, Leeds; museum, open all year

'Of all the Cistercian abbeys of England,' wrote Pevsner, 'Kirkstall is the one whose remaining buildings stand up highest. It requires little imagination to place roofs ... on the monastic buildings round the cloister and visualize the grey complex group as it must have appeared at the completion.' That was *c*1175. Even today, amid the surrounding press of Leeds, Kirkstall is a magnificent ruin. Its gatehouse is now the tea-room of the visitor centre across the road. The Abbey sits in a park, its dark stone lurking by the River Aire.

The Abbey was founded by a Norman landowner who vowed that if he recovered from an illness he would finance an outpost of Fountains Abbey on this spot. Kirkstall flourished from the 12th century until the Dissolution. It then found favour among enthusiasts for romantic ruins, being saved for the people of Leeds as early as 1889. As at Fountains and Rievaulx, the sheer scale of the ruins left much of the residential quarters still standing.

Of the residential buildings, the cloister forms the focus. The Chapter House remains to its roofline with round-headed Norman doorway and a rib-vaulted chamber beneath. The monks' dormitory stands to its full height. In the Abbot's Lodgings, the fireplaces survive, as does the Refectory along the south side of the cloister. There are service rooms beneath. The cloister wall has a charming lavatorium.

Lotherton hall

✫✫ Regency house re-modelled during the late-Victorian and Edwardian eras

At Aberford, 3 miles NE of Garforth; museum, open part year

Lotherton Hall and Park were purchased by the Gascoignes of Harewood in 1825. This unremarkable Regency property was remodelled by Colonel and Mrs Gascoigne at the end of the 19th century, reflecting the outlook and pursuits of a late Victorian family. They were committed in equal measure to the Empire, sport and fashion. The house was passed by their son, the diplomat Sir Alvary Gascoigne, and his second wife Lorna, to the City of Leeds in 1968.

The house exterior is grey, austere and unappealing. The interior is the opposite, colourful and enjoyable with a diverting collection of eccentric clutter. The tone is set by a Batoni painting of an 18th-century Gascoigne, and a table by William Burges which is covered in *objets trouvés*. Ceiling and staircase are in the style of the 17th century. Indeed, everything at Lotherton tends to be 'style of'. The drawing room is Adam revival, the boudoir Greek revival and the library Jacobean revival.

The rooms are crowded with family portraits, ceramics, antiquities and furniture, catholic if conventional in taste. They run the gamut from Grand Tour to British Empire, with a particular affection for Africa. In the dining room, pride of place goes to Edward Hughes's painting of Laura Gascoigne and her son, Alvary, an epitome of Victorian sweetness. It contrasts with an eerie portrait of the future Edward VIII, in jersey and cloth cap and with a Norwich terrier.

Upstairs, the British Empire theme continues with various bedrooms named after the colonies that Colonel Gascoigne had visited. Despite ubiquitous labels on every object – denying the boast that the house is 'as the Gascoignes left things' – this is a warm, intriguing house.

Below Many pieces on display at Lotherton have been brought in by the City of Leeds since it took over ownership in 1968. The chandelier in the Drawing Room was installed by the Gascoignes, however, and they had the green silk damask put on the walls in 1903.

Above The Top Hall at Nostell, designed by Robert Adam, features the plasterwork of the younger Joseph Rose. Wheelbacked chairs by Thomas Chippendale, decorated with the crest of the Winn family, are perfectly set against the cream-white walls. They are almost identical to chairs lining the entrance hall at Harewood House (see page 166).

Nostell priory

★ ★ ★ ☆ Paine mansion with Adam rooms and Chippendale furniture

6 miles SE of Wakefield; National Trust, open part year

Nostell is a Grand Tour project, built by a local architect, Colonel Moyser, and then by James Paine for Sir Rowland Winn. It was started *c*1733, after the money flowed on Winn's marriage to the rich daughter of a London Lord Mayor. It was continued by Paine's rival, Robert Adam, for Sir Rowland's son after 1765. Much of the interest of the house derives from a contrast between these two eras and architects.

The house was intended to have a main block with four pavilions leading from its corners, a Palladian plan executed at Holkham Hall (Norfolk). It did not turn out that way. Just the main block was completed when everything came to a halt with the younger Sir Rowland's death in a road accident in 1785. The house is virtually as he left it.

Nostell remained the seat of the Winns until the Great War. In 1914, it saw 600 employees and friends entertained on the lawn, one of the much-vaunted 'last scenes' of the traditional country house. The Winns moved away but never abandoned the place. One kept his biplane on the drive and another, the 4th Lord St Oswald, became a prominent Conservative politician. The house was given by him with fine pictures and furniture to the National Trust in 1953. The family continues to occupy part of it today.

The plan is rectangular, with two stairs at the ends of the central reception rooms rather than one in the middle. The formal upper entrance hall is set on the *piano nobile* but everyday entry is into the stone lower entrance hall, the so-called 'rustic'. Here the visitor would encounter children, servants, animals and mud. The hall today exhibits a copy of Holbein's *Sir Thomas More and his family*, the embodiment of Tudor domesticity.

The South Staircase is by Paine, with Rococo plasterwork by Joseph Rose. It leads into Adam's Top Hall. This is one of his most serene creations. Creamy white and coffee plasterwork is a rare work by Rose's son, also Joseph, in 1774–6. It is in delicate contrast to his father's work on the stairs. Wall panels, ceiling and alcove are filled with Roman motifs, the alcove a swirl of geometrical illusion. The Georgians needed no computer programmes to achieve these glorious patterns. Round the walls are wheelbacked chairs by Thomas Chippendale.

The contrast between stairs and hall, between early and mid-Georgian, is repeated in many of the state rooms. The Crimson Room has a voluptuous bed probably by Paine and a Chippendale clothes press with serpentine front. The state bedroom and dressing room are filled with Chippendale's chinoiserie. Beds, tables, chairs and wallpapers shimmer in green and gold. Trees seem to dance and birds dart across the walls.

The state dining room is mostly by Paine and the elder Rose. Its chimneypiece is richly Baroque and pictures have fussy surrounds. In the ceiling, Ceres, goddess of plenty, presides over a cornucopia. Adam clearly found this too vulgar and decorated the wall panels with delicate arabesques.

Adam's saloon matches his adjacent Top Hall. Its ceiling is alive with fans and faded pastel shades. The walls carry four Zucchi panels of pastoral scenes. The library spills over into the adjacent billiard room. Books frown from on high. Adam originally insisted on no library carpet, since the resulting dust 'is not at all good in a book room'. He also opposed drapes in dining rooms as they harboured smells. The library desk and shell-like medal cabinet are both Chippendale masterpieces. Of the remaining rooms, the drawing room is host to Angelica Kauffmann's painting of herself trying to decide a career in music or painting. She chose painting.

The celebrated Nostell dolls' house can be seen in the Museum Room downstairs. It almost merits an entry here of its own. Given the National Trust's aversion to putting figures of people in its rooms, it is ironic that the dolls' house is full of them.

Temple Newsam

5 miles E of Leeds; museum, open all year

Temple Newsam is a place of which Leeds can be proud. The house sits in a spacious park outside the city, its avenues stretching in all directions. Cooling towers, pylons and motorways may intrude on the view from the courtyard, but nothing can detract from the architectural magnificence. This ranks with Crewe Hall (Cheshire) among the great Jacobean houses of the North.

Sir Arthur Ingram was a new man of 17th-century England, a banker and tax gatherer with five properties in Yorkshire. In 1622 he bought and rebuilt the palace previously occupied by Lord Darcy and Lord Darnley, both courtiers who had lost their heads under the Tudors. Ingram refashioned Temple Newsam round three sides of a courtyard. In the parapet he wrote his homily: 'All Glory and Praise be given to God the Father the Son and Holy Ghost on High, Peace on Earth, Good Will towards Men, Honour and true Allegiance to our gracious King, Loving Affection amongst his Subjects, Health and Plenty be within this House'. That must have covered everyone and everything.

The house was handed down through the Ingram family who were created Viscounts Irwin, and survived through lateral lines and wealthy marriages well into the 20th century. Each generation luckily sought to re-interpret rather than destroy the past. Rooms were remodelled rather than wings added afresh. Such was the precision of the renovation that it is nowadays near impossible to know what is 17th, 18th, 19th or 20th century. The statesman, Lord Halifax, inherited the house between the wars. He regrettably dispersed the contents when the house went to Leeds Corporation in 1922.

The external form of the house remains largely as built, with the addition of a pretty cupola in the centre. The interiors, apart from those that are obviously Georgian, are almost entirely Jacobean reproduction or revival, commissioned by the formidable women who dominate the Temple Newsam story.

Thus the Great Hall is by an Irwin daughter, Lady Hertford, in 1820s Jacobean revival. The Elizabethan Oak Staircase was installed by Mrs Meynell Ingram in 1888, to designs by the

Right The ground floor of the south wing at Temple Newsam has a lovely enfilade of rooms. This view looks towards the Dining Room from the Edwardian Library, created in 1912 for Lord Halifax by Lenygon's of Old Burlington Street, a fashionable London firm of interior decorators. Rebuilding of this wing was begun by Frances, Lady Irwin, in the 1790s, and her daughter, the Marchioness of Hertford, redecorated most of the rooms in the 1820s.

'Temple Newsam is a **place** of which **Leeds** can be **proud.**'

Pre-Raphaelite follower, C. E. Kempe. Beyond the Hall is a lovely enfilade of rooms created in the 1820s by Lady Hertford, partly with wallpaper and fittings given by her admirer, the then Prince of Wales. To the paper in the Chinese Drawing Room she added exotic birds cut from Audubon's *Birds of America*, a favourite 19th-century decorative habit.

Temple Newsam's grand saloon is now the picture gallery. Flooded with light on both sides, it is decorated with heavy green flock wallpaper. The gallery is hung with Old Masters. Of 400 that were recorded as being in the house in the 19th century, 200 have been re-acquired, forty of them returned to their original positions in the gallery. This is a most impressive exercise in artistic rescue.

Above The already ornately patterned wallpaper in the Chinese Drawing Room is further embellished with Audubon images of birds, cut from ornithological prints. These were added by Lady Hertford in around 1827.
Right Lady Hertford's mother, Lady Irwin, chose a Gothic-style 'pillar-and-arch' wallpaper for her main bedroom. A wealthy heiress, Lady Irwin redecorated the room soon after her arrival at Temple Newsam in 1758.

Wakefield: Clarke hall

⭐ Jacobean house refurnished in original style

Aberford Road, Wakefield; museum, open by arrangement

Clarke Hall, in a Wakefield suburb, was probably built in 1680 for Benjamin Clarke, local agent for the Duke of Norfolk. He reconstructed his wife's childhood home, Bradford Hall, using local brick. The E-plan was old-fashioned for its date but fragments of the old hall have been retained in the interior.

Clarke Hall was inhabited until 1969 and then passed to the local council. It is now furnished as it would have been in Clarke's day. It is aimed specifically at children who are encouraged to dress up and immerse themselves in the daily life and work of the house. Borrowed fittings and furnishings lend authenticity. Cheese is made in the dairy. Fabric is woven in the loom room. A fire is lit in the kitchen and chickens roast on the spit.

The exterior is sober, with projecting canted bays for the principal rooms. The Great Hall runs from front to back, with symmetrical windows and doors on both sides. A chunky dining table has pride of place in front of a fire and a staircase with a 17th-century flatwork balustrade rises from one corner. Beyond is the dining room with a bizarre ceiling for a house of this size, so low it is difficult to appreciate its lavish plasterwork which spills vegetation from a central roundel. The furniture is excellent, the sideboards filled with china and pewter.

Above The grounds at Clarke Hall appear slightly distorted when viewed through the rippled glass panes of the mullioned windows. The garden design is based on 17th-century principles, as described in William Lawson's *English Housewife's Garden* of 1679.

Glossary

The aim in this book has been to avoid terms not familiar to the lay person. However, some specialist terms in common use in architectural circles may have crept in, for which the following definitions may be helpful.

acanthus – pattern of an exotic Mediterranean flower with large leaves used in classical decoration.

anthemion – a honeysuckle flower pattern used in classical decoration.

Artisan Mannerist – buildings created by masons using pattern books (rather than architects) in the period c.1615–75. Mannerism originated in 16th-century Italy and was characterised by Classical elements used in unusual ways. It was taken up in the Low Countries, then spread to England.

ashlar – any block of masonry fashioned into a wall, either load-bearing or covering brick.

bailey, inner and outer – a fortified enclosure, usually moated and surrounded by a curtain wall, containing a motte (mound) on which stands a keep. Walls are topped by battlements, with crenellations which protected defenders from arrows, and machicolations, or floor openings, through which missiles could be fired down on attackers.

baluster – upright post supporting the handrail on stairs.

bargeboard – wooden board protecting the eaves of a roof.

bay – a space of wall between any vertical element, such as an upright beam, pillar or a division into a window or door.

bay window – window projecting out from a flat wall, either canted if the sides are straight, or bowed if curved.

bolection mould – moulding concealing the join of vertical and horizontal surfaces, shaped like an S in cross-section.

Boulle – elaborate inlay work on the surface of furniture, customary in 17th and 18th-century French work.

bow – see bay window

canted – see bay window

cartouche – frame for a picture or statue, often oval and surrounded by a scroll.

caryatid – a column in the shape of a draped female figure.

casements – see sashes

chinoiserie – a style of advanced Rococo with Chinese motifs, often associated with Gothick.

coffering – a ceiling composed of beams enclosing sunken square or round panels.

collars – see roof timbers

corbel – a stone or wood projection in a wall that supports a beam, statue or window sill.

cornice – (1) a ledge or projecting upper part of a classical entablature. (2) Moulding at the top of a wall concealing the join with the ceiling.

cottage ornée – late-Georgian/Victorian picturesque cottage, usually with thatched roof and Gothic windows.

crenellation – see bailey

cruck – a simple structure of two, usually curved, trunks of wood formed into an inverted V which support the walls and roof of a medieval house.

curtain wall – in castle-building, a wall constructed between defensive projections such as bastions.

dressing – a general term for finishings; stone is dressed to either a smooth or ornamental surface.

enfilade – a line of rooms in sequence along one side of a house, usually with interconnecting doors.

entablature – a feature of classical architecture comprising everything above column height, formally composed of architrave, frieze and cornice.

flatwork – decorative plaster or woodwork in low relief.

frontispiece – a decorative bay above a doorway in a Tudor or Jacobean building, customarily composed of Renaissance motifs.

gable – the triangular end of a double-pitched roof, sometimes with stepped or scrolled (Dutch) sides.

garderobe – privy or lavatory, usually discharging into a ditch or moat outside a medieval house.

Great Chamber – see solar

grisaille – monochrome painting, usually a mural and in shades of grey.

grotesque – decorative wall motif of human figures, as found in Roman grottoes.

half-timbering – term for timber-framed house derived from the practice of splitting logs in half to provide beams.

hipped roof – a roof with a sloping end instead of an end gable.

Ho-Ho bird – chinoiserie motif associated with 18th-century Rococo style.

jetty or jettied floor – upper floor extended, or oversailed, beyond the lower one to give more space upstairs and to protect the lower walls from adverse weather. Jettying also uses the downward thrust of the upper walls to form a cantilever, preventing internal ceiling beams from bowing.

keep – see bailey

king post – see roof timbers

linenfold – a pattern on wall panels imitating folded linen.

louvre – a covered turret above a medieval hall that allowed smoke to escape.

machicolation – see bailey

mansard – a roof with two separate pitches of slope.

motte – see bailey

mullion – central divider of window, made of metal or stone.

oversail – see jetty

oriel – an upper window projecting from a wall, sometimes (incorrectly) used to indicate a tall medieval window lighting the dais end of the Great Hall.

Palladian – a style of classical architecture, formal and refined outside, often lavish inside, named after Italian architect, Andrea Palladio (1508–80). Moving spirit behind most English classical designers, especially Inigo Jones and, later, Lord Burlington, William Kent and the early Georgians.

parlour – see solar

piano nobile – the main ceremonial floor of a classical building, sitting on the basement or 'rustic' lower floor.

pier-glass – a wall mirror supported by a small table, bracket or console.

pilaster – a flat column projecting only slightly from a wall.

pointing – mortar or cement used to seal between bricks.

porte-cochère – a grand porch with a driveway through it, allowing passengers to alight from carriages under cover.

prodigy house – a large, ostentatious house of the Elizabethan/Jacobean period.

putti – unwinged sculptures of chubby boys found in Classical and Baroque decoration.

queen post – see roof timbers

quoins – dressed corner stones.

render – a covering of stucco, cement or limewash on the outside of a building.

Rococo – the final phase of Baroque style in the 18th century, typified by refined painted and plaster decoration, often asymmetrical and with figures.

roof timbers – a tie-beam runs horizontally across the roof space; a king post rises vertically from the tie beam to the apex of the roof; queen posts rise not to the apex but to subsidiary beams known as collars; wind-braces strengthen the roof rafters.

rustic – a name given in Palladian architecture to the lower floor or basement, beneath the piano nobile.

rustication – treatment of ashlar by deep-cutting joints so they look stronger or cruder.

sashes – windows opening by rising on sash ropes or cords, as opposed to casements which open on side hinges.

scagliola – composition of artificial stone that imitates appearance of grained marble.

screens passage – accessed from the main door of a medieval building and built into one end of a Great Hall to shield it from draughts. Door ors arches lead from the passage into the hall on one side and kitchens on other. Above is usually a minstrels' gallery.

Serlian – motifs derived from pattern books of the Italian Renaissance architect, Sebastiano Serlio (1475–1554).

sgraffito – plaster decoration scratched to reveal another colour beneath.

solar – the upstairs room at the family end of a medieval hall, originally above an undercroft or parlour. Originally accessed by ladder or spiral stairs, it was usually replaced by a Great Chamber in the Tudor era.

strapwork – strap or ribbon-like decorative scrolls in Elizabethan and Jacobean design.

stucco – plaster, usually protective, covering for brick, sometimes fashioned to look like stone.

studding – vertical timbers laid close to each other to strengthen the wall. Close-studding tends to indicate wealth.

tie-beam – see roof timbers

undercroft – a vaulted room or crypt beneath a building, partly or wholly underground

vault – a ceiling, usually of stone composed of arches.

Venetian window – Palladian window composed of three components, the centre one arched.

wind-braces – see roof timbers

Simon Jenkins sources

The best guides to any house are the people who occupy it. They have felt its walls and sensed its seasons. They stand witness to its ghosts, real and imagined, and have thus become part of its history. As a substitute, guidebooks vary widely from the academic to the plain childish. The best are published by English Heritage, erudite and enjoyable. National Trust guidebooks are at last moving from the scholarly to the accessible, and the Trust's compendium *Guide*, by Lydia Greeves and Michael Trinick, is excellent.

My selection of a thousand properties derives from numerous sources. These include Hudson's *Historic Houses and Gardens*, supplemented by *Museums and Galleries* published by Tomorrow's Guides. The Historic Houses Association website is another invaluable source. Of recent house surveys, the best are John Julius Norwich's *Architecture of Southern England* (1985), John Martin Robinson's *Architecture of Northern England* (1986) and Hugh Montgomery-Massingberd's *Great Houses of England and Wales* (2000). Nigel Nicolson's *Great Houses of Britain* (1978) describes the most prominent. Their lists are not exhaustive and include houses not open to the public. Behind them stands Nikolaus Pevsner's massive 'Buildings of England' series, which deals with houses more generously (with plans) in the newer revised editions.

On English domestic architecture, the classics are hard to beat. They include Olive Cook's *The English House Through Seven Centuries* (1968), Alec Clifton-Taylor's *The Pattern of English Building* (1972), Hugh Braun's *Old English Houses* (1962), Sacheverell Sitwell's *British Architects and Craftsmen* (1964) and Plantagenet Somerset Fry's *Castles of Britain and Ireland* (1980).

On specific periods the best are Mark Girouard's *Robert Smythson and the English Country House* (1983), Giles Worsley's *Classical Architecture in England* (1995), Kerry Downes's *English Baroque Architecture* (1966) and Girouard's *The Victorian Country House* (1971). Joe Mordaunt Crook takes a lively look at the Victorian battle of the styles in *The Dilemma of Style* (1989). Jeremy Musson describes the manorial revival in *The English Manor House* (1999) and Gavin Stamp takes a wider look at the same period in *The English House 1860–1914* (1986). *Edwardian Architecture*, edited by Alastair Service (1975), brings the story into the 20th century and Clive Aslet's *The Last Country Houses* (1982) almost completes it.

On social history, Girouard's *Life in the English Country House* (1978) is incomparable. *Creating Paradise* (2000) by Richard Wilson and Alan Mackley sets the house in its economic context. So does Mordaunt Crook's *The Rise of the Nouveaux Riches* (1999) and David Cannadine's *The Decline and Fall of the British Aristocracy* (1990). Adrian Tinniswood offers a fascinating insight in his *History of Country House Visiting* (1989). The desperate post-war bid to save houses is described in Marcus Binney's *Our Vanishing Heritage* (1984) and John Cornforth's *The Country Houses of England 1948–1998* (1998). Peter Mandler covers the same period in his scholarly *The Fall and Rise of the Stately Home* (1997).

Biographies of architects are too legion to list but Howard Colvin's *Biographical Dictionary of British Architects* (1978) was my bible over disputed dates and attributions. Of a more personal character is James Lees-Milne's delightful account of the National Trust's early acquisitions in *People and Places* (1992). Houses in distress are visited in John Harris's *No Voice from the Hall* (1998). *Writers and their Houses* (1993) is a first-class collection of essays, edited by Kate Marsh.

I am indebted to the many architectural commentaries in *Country Life*, champion of the historic buildings cause for over a century. I do not believe I could have found a thousand houses for my list were it not for its progenitors, Edward Hudson and Christopher Hussey, and their many successors.

Contact details

Aske Hall – The Marquess of Zetland, Richmond, North Yorks, DL10 5HJ www.aske.co.uk Tel 01748 822000 Open to public only on specific days, dates shown on website; group tours by appointment, Mon–Fri 10am–3pm

Bar Convent Museum – Bar Convent Trust, 17 Blossom St, York, YO24 1AQ www.bar-convent.org.uk Tel 01904 643238 Open Mon–Fri (except BHs), museum & convent tours at 10.30am & 2.30pm, contact for other openings

Barden Tower – Tourism Dept, Estate Office, Bolton Abbey, Skipton, North Yorks, BD23 6EX tourism@boltonabbey.com Tel 01756 718009 Open to view exterior at any reasonable time

Barley Hall – 2 Coffee Yard, off Stonegate, York, YO1 8AR www.barleyhall.org.uk Tel 01904 610276 Open Tue–Sun (& BH Mon) 10am–4pm

Beningbrough Hall – National Trust, Beningbrough, North Yorks, YO30 1DD www.nationaltrust.org.uk/main/placestovisit Tel 01904 470666 Open 12th Mar–26th Jun, Sat to Wed; 27th Jun–28th Aug, daily except Thur; 29th Aug–30th Oct, Sat–Wed; hall 12–5pm, grounds 11am–5.30pm

Bishop's House, Sheffield – Sheffield Galleries and Museums Trust, Norton Lees Lane, Sheffield, S8 9BE www.sheffieldgalleries.org.uk Tel 0114 278 2600 Open Sat 10am–4.30pm, Sun 11am–4.30pm; pre-booked educational groups Mon–Fri 10am–3pm

Bolling Hall, Bradford – Bowling Hall Road, Bradford, BD4 7LP www.visitbradford.com Tel 01274 723057 Open Wed–Fri & BH Mon 11am–4pm, Sat 10am–5pm, Sun 12–5pm

Bolton Castle – Lord Bolton, Leyburn, North Yorks, DL8 4ET www.boltoncastle.co.uk Tel 01969 623981 Open daily Apr–Sep, 10am–5pm; Oct–Mar, 10–4pm (or dusk)

Bramham Park – Nick Lane-Fox, Bramham, Nr Wetherby, West Yorks, LS23 6ND www.bramhampark.co.uk Tel 01937 846005 Group tours of house by arrangement; gardens open 1st Apr–30th Sep, 11.30am–4.30pm (may be closed for special events)

Brockfield Hall – Mr & Mrs Simon Wood, Warthill, York, YO19 5XJ Tel 01904 489362 Open 31 Jul and Aug, daily except Mon (open BH Mon), 1–4pm; open by appointment at other times

Brodsworth Hall – English Heritage, Brodsworth, Nr Doncaster, Yorks, DN5 7XJ www.english-heritage.org.uk/yorkshire Tel 01302 722598 House open 19th Mar–2nd Oct, Tue–Sun & BH Mon, 1–5pm; 3rd–31st Oct, Sat & Sun 12–4pm; gardens open 19th Mar–31st Oct, daily, 10am–6pm

Brontë Parsonage, Haworth – The Brontë Society, Church Street, Haworth, Keighley, West Yorks, BD22 8DR www.bronte.info Tel 01535 642323 Open Apr–Sep, 10am–5pm; Oct–Mar, 11am–4.30pm

Broughton Hall – The Tempest Family, Skipton, North Yorks, BD23 3AE www.broughtonhall.co.uk Tel 01756 799608 Tours by arrangement

Burton Agnes Hall – Burton Agnes Hall Preservation Trust, Burton Agnes, Driffield, East Yorks, YO25 OND www.burton-agnes.com Tel 01262 490324 Open daily 1st Apr–31st Oct, 11am–5pm

Burton Agnes Manor House – English Heritage, Burton Agnes, Driffield, East Yorks www.english-heritage.org.uk/yorkshire Open daily 1st Apr–31st Oct, 11am–5pm

Burton Constable Hall – Burton Constable Foundation, Skirlaugh, East Yorks, HU11 4LN www.burtonconstable.com Tel 01964 562400 Open Easter Sat to 31st Oct; Sat to Thur, hall 1–5pm, grounds & tearoom 12.30–5pm

Cannon Hall – Barnsley Metropolitan Borough Council, Cawthorne, Barnsley, South Yorks, S75 4AT www.barnsley.gov.uk Tel 01226 790270 Open Apr–Oct, Wed–Fri 10.30am–5pm, Sat & Sun12–5pm; Nov, Dec & Mar, Sun 12–4pm

Carlton Towers – Carlton, North Yorks, DN14 9LZ www.carltontowers.co.uk Tel 01405 861662 Open by arrangement

Castle Howard – The Hon Simon Howard, York, North Yorks YO60 7DA www.castlehoward.co.uk Tel 01653 648333 Open daily 1st Mar–6th Nov, 10am–4pm; from Nov to mid Feb grounds only

Clarke Hall, Wakefield – Aberford Road, Wakefield, Wakefield, WF1 4AL www.clarke-hall.co.uk Tel 01924 302700 Open by arrangement in term time

Cliffe Castle, Keighley – City of Bradford Metropolitan District Council, Spring Gardens Lane, Keighley, West Yorks, BD20 6LH Tel 01535 618231 Open by arrangement

Clifford's Tower – English Heritage, Tower Street, York, YO1 9SA www.english-heritage.org.uk/yorkshire Tel 01904 646940 Open 19th Mar–30th Sep 10am–6pm; 1st–31st Oct 10am–5pm, 1st Nov–31st Mar 10am–4pm

Conigsbrough Castle – English Heritage, Castle Hill, Conigsbrough, South Yorks, DN12 3BU www.english-heritage.org.uk/yorkshire Tel 01709 863329 Open daily 1st Apr–30th Sep 10am–5pm; 1st Oct–31st Mar 10am–4pm

Constable Burton Hall – M.C.A Wyvill Esq, Leyburn, North Yorks, DL8 5LJ www.constableburtongardens.co.uk Tel 01677 450428 Gardens only, open daily 19th Mar–16th Oct, 9am–6pm

Crathorne Hall – Crathorne, Yarm, North Yorks, TS15 0AR Tel 01642 700398 (hotel)

Cusworth Hall, Doncaster – The Museum of South Yorkshire Life, Cusworth Lane, Doncaster, DN5 7TU www.doncaster.gov.uk Tel 01302 782342 Undergoing restoration, contact museum for opening times; grounds open

Duncombe Park – Lord & Lady Feversham, Helmsley, North Yorks, YO62 5EB www.duncombepark.com Tel 01439 770213 Open 1st May–30th Oct, Sun–Thur; house by guided tours at 12.30, 1.30, 2.30 & 3.30pm; gardens and parkland 11am–5.30pm

East Riddlesden Hall, Keighley – National Trust, Bradford Road, Keighley, West Yorks, BD20 5EL www.nationaltrust.org.uk Tel 01535 607075 Open 19th Mar–6th Nov, Tue, Wed, Sat & Sun (& Mon 3rd Sept–6th Nov) 12–5pm

Fairfax House – York Civic Trust, 27 Castlegate, York, YO1 9RN www.fairfaxhouse.co.uk Tel 01904 655543 Open 5th Feb–31st Dec; Mon–Thur & Sat, 11am–5pm; Fri, tours at 11am & 2pm; Sun, 1.30–5pm

The Folly, Settle – North Craven Building Preservation Trust, The Folly & Museum of North Craven Life, c/o 6 Chapel St, Settle, BD24 9HS www.ncbpt.org.uk and www.settle.org.uk Tel 01524 251388 Open 10.30am–4.30pm Easter, May & Aug BH weekends (plus Tue) and 1st July–30th Sep. Also open on other occasions, ring to check. Ground flour of north wing available for holiday lets www.the-folly.co.uk Tel 0870 1917700

Fountains Abbey & Fountains Hall – National Trust, Ripon, North Yorks, HG4 3DY www.fountainsabbey.org.uk Tel 01765 608888 Open daily Mar–Oct, 10am–5pm; Nov–Feb, 10am–4pm

Harewood House – The Earl of Harewood, Harewood, Leeds, West Yorks, LS17 9LQ www.harewood.org Tel 0113 218 1010 Open daily, 4th Feb–6th Nov 10am–6pm; gardens only, 7th Nov–11th Dec, Sat & Sun

Hazelwood Castle – Paradise Lane, Hazelwood, Tadcaster, North Yorks, LS24 9NJ www.hazelwood-castle.co.uk Tel 01937 535353 (hotel)

Helmsley Castle – English Heritage, Castlegate, Helmsley, N Yorks YO62 5AB www.english-heritage.org.uk/yorkshire Tel 01439 770442 Open daily 19th Mar–30th Sep, 10am–6pm; 1st Oct–31st Mar, Thurs–Mon 10am–4pm

Holdsworth House, Halifax – Holdsworth, Halifax, West Yorks, HX2 9TG www.holdsworthhouse.co.uk Tel 01422 240024 (hotel)

House in the Rock, Knaresborough – Currently for sale. www.knaresborough.co.uk or www.harrogate.gov.uk View from Low Bridge Gardens, park on corner of Low Bridge and Abbey Road

House of Correction, Ripon – Ripon Museum Trust, St Marygate, Ripon, North Yorks www.riponmusuems.co.uk Tel 01765 690799 Open daily, 19th Mar–31st Oct, 1–4pm (11am–4pm during local school holidays)

Hovingham Hall – William Worsley, Hovingham, York, North Yorks, YO62 4LU www.hovingham.co.uk Tel 01653 628771 Open daily except Sun 31st May–11th June & 20th June–9th July, 12.30–4.30pm

James Herriot's house, Thirsk – The World of James Herriot, 23 Kirkgate, Thirsk, North Yorks, YO7 1PL www.hambleton.gov.uk Tel 01845 524234 Open daily, Apr–Oct, 10am–6pm; Nov–Mar, 11am–4pm

Jorvik Viking Centre – York Archaeological Trust, Coppergate, York YO1 9WT www.jorvik-viking-centre.co.uk Tel 01904 643211 Open daily April–Oct, 10am–5pm, Nov–Mar, 10am–4pm (9am–5pm during school holidays)

The King's Manor – York University, Exhibition Square (behind Museum St), York www.york.ac.uk/admin/presspr/kmanor

Kiplin Hall – Kiplin Hall Trustees, Kiplin, Nr Scorton, Richmond, North Yorks DL10 6AT www.kiplinhall.co.uk Open 2–5pm on Sun, Tue & BH Mon in Easter weekend, May & Sept; Sun–Wed in Jun, July & Aug

Kirkstall Abbey, Leeds – Abbey Walk, Kirkstall Road, Leeds, LS5 3EH www.leeds.gov.uk Tel 0113 230 5492 Open dawn to dusk all year

Longley Old Hall, Huddersfield – Robin & Christine Gallagher, Longley, Huddersfield, HD5 8LB www.longleyoldhall.co.uk Tel 01484 430852 Open for pre-booked guided tours

Lotherton Hall – Leeds City Council, Aberford, West Yorks, LS25 3EB www.leeds.gov.uk Tel 0113 281 3259 Open 1st Apr–31st Oct, Tue–Sat 10am–5pm, Sun 1–5pm; 1st Nov–31st Dec & Mar, Tue–Sat 10am–4pm, Sun 12–4pm

Maister House, Hull – National Trust, 160 High Street, Hull, East Yorks, HU1 1NL www.nationaltrust.org.uk/main/placestovisit Tel 01482 324114 Open daily except Sat & Sun, 10am–4pm, stairwell only

Mansion House, Doncaster – Doncaster City Council, High Street, Doncaster, DN1 1BN www.doncaster.gov.uk Tel 01302 734032 Open to group tours by arrangement; an open day is held in summer

Mansion House, York – St Helen's Square, York www.york.gov.uk Tel 01904 551049 Open Mar to Christmas, guided tours Fri & Sat, 11am & 2pm

Markenfield Hall – Lady Deirdre Curteis, Nr Ripon, North Yorks, HG4 3AD www.markenfield.com Tel 01765 603411 Open daily 1st–14th May & 19th Jun–1st Jul, 2–5pm; groups all year by appointment

Marmion Tower – English Heritage, Church Street, West Tanfield, North Yorks www.english-heritage.org.uk/yorkshire Open daily, 24th Mar–30 Sep 10am–6pm; 1st–31st Oct 10am–5pm; 1st Nov–31st Mar 10am–4pm

Merchant Adventurers' Hall – The York Company, Fossgate, York, YO1 9XD www.theyorkcompany.co.uk Tel 01904 654818 Open Apr–Sep, Mon–Thur 9am–5pm, Fri–Sat 9am–3.30pm, Sun 12–4pm; Oct–Mar, 9am–3.30pm

Middleham Castle – English Heritage, Castle Hill, Middleham, Leyburn, North Yorks, DL8 4QR www.english-heritage.org.uk/yorkshire Tel 01969 623899 Open daily 19th Mar–30th Sep, 10am–6pm; 1st Oct–31st Mar, Thur–Mon 10am–4pm

Middlethorpe Hall – Bishopthorpe Road, York, YO23 2GB www.middlethorpe.com Tel 01904 641241 (hotel)

Moulton Hall – National Trust, Moulton, Richmond, North Yorks, DL10 6QH www.nationaltrust.org.uk/main/placestovisit Tel 01325 377227 Open by arrangement with the tenant, Viscount Eccles

Mount Grace Priory – English Heritage, Staddlebridge, Nr Northallerton, North Yorks, DL6 3JG www.english-heritage.org.uk/yorkshire Tel 01609 883494 Open daily 19th Mar–30th Sep, 10am–6pm; 1st Oct–31st Mar, Thur–Mon 10am–4pm

Newburgh Priory – Sir George Wombwell Bt, Coxwold, North Yorks, YO61 4AS www.newburghpriory.co.uk Tel 01347 868435 Open 27th Mar–29th Jun, Wed & Sun (also Easter Sun & Mon), house 2.30–4.45pm, garden 2–6pm

Newby Hall – Mr Richard Compton, Ripon, North Yorks, HG4 5AE www.newbyhall.com Tel 01423 322583 Open 25th Mar–2nd Oct, Tue–Sun & BH Mon (daily Jul & Aug), house 12–5pm, gardens 11am–5pm

Norton Conyers – Sir James and Lady Graham, Nr Ripon, North Yorks, HG4 5EQ Tel 01765 640333 Open 27th–28th Mar, 1st–2nd & 29th–30th May, 27th Jun–2nd Jul, 28th–29th Aug, house 2–5pm, gardens 12–4.30pm (Thur 10am–4pm)

Nostell Priory – National Trust, Doncaster Road, Wakefield, West Yorks, WF4 1QE www.nationaltrust.org.uk/main/placestovisit Tel 01924 863892 House open 19th Mar–6th Nov, Wed–Sun 1–5pm; 3rd–11th Dec, daily 11am–5pm; grounds open 5th–20th Mar, Sat & Sun 11am–5pm; 23rd Mar–6th Nov, Wed–Sun 11am–6pm; 3rd–11th Dec, daily 11am–4.30pm

Nunnington Hall – National Trust, Nunnington, North Yorks, YO62 5UY www.nationaltrust.org.uk/main/placestovisit Tel 01439 748283 Open 12th Mar–30th Apr, 1st–30th Oct, Wed–Sun 1.30–5pm; 1st May–30th Sep, Wed–Sun (also Tue, 31st May–31st Aug) 1.30–5.30pm

Oakwell Hall, Gomersal – Nutter Lane, Birstall, Batley, WF17 9LG www.oakwellhallcountrypark.co.uk Tel 01924 326240 Open Mon–Fri 11am–5pm, Sat–Sun 12–5pm

Ormesby Hall – National Trust, Ladgate Lane, Ormesby, Middlesbrough, TS7 9AS www.nationaltrust.org.uk/main/placestovisit Tel 01642 324188 Open 25th Mar–31st Oct, Fri–Mon 1.30–5pm

Red House, Gomersal – Oxford Road, Gomersal, BD19 4JP www.redhousemuseum.co.uk Tel 01274 335100 Open Mon–Fri 11am–5pm, Sat–Sun 12–5pm

Richmond Castle – English Heritage, Tower St, Richmond, North Yorks, DL10 4QW www.english-heritage.org.uk/yorkshire Tel 01748 822493 Open daily 19th Mar–30th Sep, 10am–6pm; 1st Oct–31st Mar, Thur–Mon 10am–4pm

Rievaulx Abbey – English Heritage, Rievaulx, Nr Helmsley, North Yorks, YO62 5LB www.english-heritage.org.uk/yorkshire Tel 01439 798228 Open daily 19th Mar–30th Sep, 10am–6pm; 1st Oct–31st Mar, Thur–Mon 10am–4pm

Rievaulx Terrace, Ionic Temple – National Trust, Rievaulx, Nr Helmsley, North Yorks, YO62 5LJ www.nationaltrust.org.uk/main/placestovisit Tel 01439 748283 Open daily 12th Mar–30th Oct, 10.30–6pm (5pm in Oct)

Ripley Castle – Sir Thomas Ingilby Bt, Ripley, Harrogate, North Yorks, HG3 3AY www.ripleycastle.co.uk Tel 01423 770152 House open 10.30am–3pm, daily in July & Aug, on Tue, Thur, Sat & Sun in Jan–June & Sep–Dec; gardens open daily 10am–5pm

Ryedale Folk Museum – The Crosland Foundation, Hutton le Hole, York, North Yorks, YO62 6UA www.ryedalefolkmuseum.co.uk Tel 01751 417367 Open 14th Mar–13th Nov, daily 10am–5.30pm

St William's College – Dean & Chapter of York, 5 College Street, York YO1 7JF www.yorkminster.org Tel 01904 557233 Open 10am–5pm

Scampston Hall – Sir Charles Legard Bt, Scampston, Malton, North Yorks, YO17 8NG www.scampston.co.uk Tel 01944 758224 Open daily except Mon, 23rd Jun–24th July, 1.30–5pm

Sewerby Hall – East Riding of Yorkshire Council, Church Lane, Sewerby, Bridlington, East Yorks, YO15 1EA www.eastriding.gov.uk/sewerby Tel 01262 673769 Hall open 12th Feb–15th Mar, Sat–Tue 11am–4.30pm; 19th Mar–30th Oct, daily 10am–5.30pm; grounds open daily, dawn to dusk

Shandy Hall – The Laurence Sterne Trust, Coxwold, North Yorks, YO61 4AD www.asterisk.org.uk Tel 01347 868465 Open 1st May–30th Sep; house Wed 2–4.30pm, Sun 2.30–4.30pm; gardens Sun–Fri 11am–4.30pm

Shibden Hall, Halifax – Calderdale Metropolitan Borough Council, Lister's Road, Halifax, West Yorks, HX3 6XG www.calderdale.gov.uk Tel 01422 352246 Open 1st Mar–30th Nov, Mon–Sat 10am–5pm, Sun 12–5pm; Dec– Feb, Mon–Sat 10am–4pm, Sun 12–4pm

Sion Hill Hall – H.W. Mawer Trust, Kirby Wiske, Thirsk, North Yorks, YO7 4EU www.sionhillhall.co.uk Tel 01845 587206 Open Wed only Jun–Sep, Easter Sun and BHs, 1–5pm. Tours May–Oct by arrangement

Skipton Castle – Skipton, North Yorks, BD23 1AQ www.skiptoncastle.co.uk Tel 01756 792442 Open all year, Mon–Sat 10am–6pm, Sun 12–6pm

Sledmere House – Sir Tatton Sykes Bt, Sledmere, Driffield, E Yorks, YO25 3XG www.sledmerehouse.com Tel 01377 236637 Open Easter 25th–28th Mar, 1st–29th Apr (grounds, shop & cafe), 30th Apr–18th Sep (closed 13th–18th June); house 11.30am–4pm, grounds & shop 10.30am–5pm, cafe 10am–5pm

Stockeld Park – Mr & Mrs P.G.F Grant, Wetherby, North Yorks, LS22 4AW Tel 01937 586101 Open by arrangement

Sutton Park – Sir Reginald & Lady Sheffield, Sutton-on-the-Forest, North Yorks, YO61 1DP www.statelyhome.co.uk Tel 01347 810249/811239 Open 25th Mar–28th Sep; house Wed, Sun & BH Mon 1.30–5pm; gardens daily 11am–5pm

Swinton Park – Swinton, Masham, North Yorks, HG4 4JH www.swintonpark.com Tel 01765 680900 (hotel)

Temple Newsam – Leeds City Council, Leeds, LS15 0AE www.leeds.gov.uk Tel 0113 264 7321 Open Tue–Sun, BH Mon & occasional events, 10.30am–5pm (4pm in winter)

Treasurer's House – National Trust, Minster Yard, York, YO1 7JL www.nationaltrust.org.uk/main/placestovisit (NB to access website, type Treasurers House, no apostrophe) Tel 01904 624247 Open daily except Fri, 16th Mar–31st Oct, 11am–4.30pm

Turner's Hospital, Kirkleatham – 1 Sir William Turner's Court, Kirkleatham, Redcar, TS10 4QT Tel 01642 482828

Union Workhouse, Ripon – Ripon Museum Trust, Allhallowgate, Ripon, North Yorks, HG1 4LE www.riponmusuems.co.uk Tel 01765 690799 Open daily, 1st Apr–26th Oct, 1–4pm (11am–4pm during local school holidays)

Wentworth Castle – Barnsley Metropolitan Borough Council, Lowe Lane, Stainborough, Barnsley, South Yorks, S75 3ET www.wentworthcastle.org Tel 01226 776040 Open 19th Mar–30th Oct, Sat & Sun 2–5pm; contact for open days and group visits

Wentworth Woodhouse – Not open. Exterior can be viewed from Trans-Pennine Way footpath near Wentworth village www.wentworthvillage.net

Whitby Banqueting house – English Heritage, Whitby, North Yorks, YO22 4JT www.english-heritage.org.uk/yorkshire Tel 01947 603568 Open daily 19th Mar–31st Oct, 10am–6pm (to 5pm in Oct); 1st Nov–31st Mar, Thur–Mon 10am–4pm

Wilberforce House, Hull – Hull City Council, 25 High Street, Hull, East Yorks, HU1 1NQ www.hullcc.gov.uk/museums Tel 01482 613902 Open Mon–Sat 10am–5pm, Sun 1.30–4pm

York Castle Museum – Eye of York, Tower Street, York, YO1 9RY www.yorkcastlemuseum.org.uk Tel 01904 687687 Open daily 9.30am–5pm

Index

Main entries for houses are in **bold**

T=top TL=top left TR=top right B=bottom BL=bottom left BR=bottom right
L=left R=right C=centre CL=centre left CR=centre right

Front Cover English Heritage/John Critchley **Back Cover** Collections/Mike Kipling
Endpapers © Leeds Museums and Galleries/(Temple Newsam House) **1** Simon Miles
Photography **2-3** Jerry Hardman-Jones **4-7** European Map Graphics Ltd. **8** Quintin Wright
10-13 © Reader's Digest/Illustrations by Hardlines Ltd **14-15** The Interior Archive/
Christopher Simon Sykes **16-18** Jarrold Publishing/Neil Jinkerson **19** Jarrold Publishing
20 English Heritage/Bob Skingle **21** David Lyons **22 T** Burton Constable Foundation
B Jarrold Publishing/Neil Jinkerson **22-23 B** Jarrold Publishing/Neil Jinkerson **24 TL** The
National Trust Yorkshire and NE Region **24-25** Jeremy Phillips **25 TR** Collections/Liz Stares
26 T www.bridgeman.co.uk/Wilberforce House, Hull City Museums & Art Galleries, UK
B Collections/McQuillan & Brown **27 T** Collections/Mike Kipling **B** Popperfoto
28-29 Collections/Mike Kipling **29** The Interior Archive/Christopher Simon Sykes
30-32 Jerry Hardman-Jones **33** Collections/Gary Smith **34** The National Trust/Niall Clutton
35 The National Trust/AndreasVonEinsiedel **36** The National Trust/Derry Moore
37 The National Trust/Andreas von Einsiedel **38** Collections/Roy Stedall-Humphryes
39 www.bridgeman.co.uk/Victoria & Albert Museum, London, UK **40** Jerry Hardman-Jones
41 T The Tempest Family **B** Jerry Hardman-Jones **42** Country Life/Simon **43 T** Country
Life/Simon Upton **B** © Reader's Digest **44** Collections/Quintin Wright **45 L** By Courtesy of
the National Portrait Gallery, London **R** From the Castle Howard Collection **46-47** David
Lyons **48 L** Skyscan **48-49** From the Castle Howard Collection **49** Yorkshire Post
Newspapers **50** Phil Robinson **51** Collections/Mike Kipling **52-53 T** Lord Feversham
B Peter Heaton **53** Lord Feversham **54 T** John Parker **B** The National Trust/Andrew Butler
55 John Parker **56** The National Trust/Matthew Antrobus **57** Hazlewood Castle
58 L Collections/Roy Stedall-Humphrys **R** English Heritage/Bob Skingle **58-59** Skyscan
60 TL Simon Miles Photography **TR** Robert Wainwright **CL** Country Life **61** Nick McCann
62 Collections/Quintin Wright **63-4** Mike Kipling Photography **65** Collections/Quintin
Wright **66-67** Paul Freeman **67** Markenfield Hall **68** English Heritage/Bob Skingle
69 L English Heritage/Andrew Tryner **R** Collections/Gary Smith **70** The National Trust/John
Bethell **71 L** Collections/Mike Kipling **R** English Heritage/Jonathan Bailey **72 T** Simon
Miles Photography **B** Sir George Wombwell Bt **73** Simon Miles Photography **74-75** Jerry
Hardman-Jones **76-79** Collections/Quintin Wright **80 T** The National Trust/Mike Williams
B Collections/Mike Kipling **81-82** The National Trust/Mike Williams **83 T** The National
Trust/Dennis Gilbert **B** The National Trust/Matthew Antrobus **84 T** Collections/Michael
Jenner **B** English Heritage **85** John Parker **86-87** The National Trust/Andrea Jones
B Collections/Michael Jenner **88-89** Simon Miles Photography **90 T** Ripon Museum Trust
B Ripon Museum Trust **90-91** Collections/Quintin Wright **91 T** Ripon Museum Trust
92-93 Ryedale Folk Museum **94-95 T** Country Life/Tim Imrie-Tait **B** Sir Charles Legard
95 Country Life/Tim Imrie-Tait **96 L** North Craven Building Preservation Trust Ltd **R** David
Alcock www.thecravenimage.co.uk **97 T** Collections/Gary Smith **B** © Laurence Sterne
Trust **98-99** © Laurence Sterne Trust **99** By Courtesy of the National Portrait Gallery,
London **100** Jerry Hardman-Jones **101 T** Sion Hill Hall **B** Jerry Hardman-Jones
102-103 Skipton Castle, Yorkshire **104 T** Courtesy of Stockeld Park **B** Simon Miles
Photography **105-107** Jerry Hardman-Jones **108** Country Life/Charlotte Winn
109 Collections/Mike Kipling **110 L** Collections/Mike Kipling **110-111** Collections/Mike
Kipling **111 T** 'Courtesy of World of James Herriot.' **B** Collections/Mike Kipling
112-113 Collections/Mike Kipling **113** Skyscan/© Flightimages **114-115**
www.jasonhawkes.com **116-117** Bar Convent Museum **118** York Archaeological Trust
119 English Heritage/Joan Blencowe **120-121** York Civic Trust **122-123** York
Archaeological Trust **124-125** University of York **126-127** York Civic Trust/Jeremy Phillips
128 T Collections/Quintin Wright **B** Collections/Quintin Wright **128-129** Jeremy Phillips
130-131 T Middlethorpe Hall. **B** Middlethorpe Hall. **131 BR** Dean and Chapter of York
132 TL The National Trust/Nick Meers **BL** The National Trust/Bill Batten **BR** The National
Trust/John Hammond **132-133 T** The National Trust/Bill Batten **134** The National Trust/Bill
Baten **135** York Museums Trust (York Castle Museum) **136-137** Doncaster Metropolitan
Borough Council Museums Service **138-139** English Heritage/John Critchley
140-141 T Barnsley Metropolitan Borough Council Cannon Hall Museum (David Sharp).
B Barnsley Metropolitan Borough Council Cannon Hall Museum (John Marshall)
141 TR By Courtesy of the National Portrait Gallery, London **142-143** English
Heritage/Keith Buck **143** Collections/Roy Stedall-Humphryes **144-145** Doncaster
Metropolitan Borough Council Museums Service **145 L** Doncaster Metropolitan Borough
Council **R** Doncaster Metropolitan Borough Council **146** Collections/Barbara West
147-149 Mark Newcombe & Paul Chave **150-151** Country Life/Paul Barker
152-155 Jerry Hardman-Jones **156-157** Jeremy Phillips **158-159** Kirklees Metropolitan
Council/Photos Patrick Crowley **160** Kirklees Metropolitan Council Culture & Leisure
Service **161** Holdsworth House **162-163 T** Shibden Hall/Photo Tony Sharpe **B** Shibden
Hall/Photo Malcolm Duncan **164-167** Jerry Hardman-Jones **68 B** By Courtesy of the
National Portrait Gallery, London **168-169** Collections/Roger Scruton **169** (c) The Bronte
Society **170-171** Jerry Hardman-Jones **172-173** Cliffe Castle Museum/David Sheldon
174-175 The National Trust/Matthew Antrobus **176-177** The National Trust/Mike Williams
176 Jerry Hardman-Jones **177 T** © Leeds Museums & Galleries/Lotherton Hall **B** © Leeds
Museums & Galleries/Lotherton Hall **178** The National Trust/Andreas von Einsiedel
179 Angelo Hornak **180-181** The National Trust/Andreas von Einsiedel **181 T** The
National Trust/Mark Fiennes **BR** Angelo Hornak **182-184** © Leeds Museums &
Galleries/Temple Newsam **185** Jerry Hardman-Jones

Discover Britain's Historic Houses: Yorkshire

Reader's Digest Project Team
Series editor Christine Noble
Art editor Jane McKenna
Picture researcher Christine Hinze
Writer Caroline Smith
Proofreader Ron Pankhurst
Indexer Marie Lorimer

Reader's Digest General Books
Editorial director Julian Browne
Art director Nick Clark
Managing editor Alastair Holmes
Picture resource manager Martin Smith
Pre-press account manager Penelope Grose

Colour origination Colour Systems Limited, London
Printed and bound in Europe by Arvato, Iberia

We are committed to both the quality of our products and
the service we provide to our customers. We value your
comments, so please feel free to contact us on **08705 113366**
or via our web site at **www.readersdigest.co.uk**

If you have any comments or suggestions about the
content of our books, you can contact us at:
gbeditorial@readersdigest.co.uk

Published by The Reader's Digest Association Limited,
11 Westferry Circus, Canary Wharf, London E14 4HE

www.readersdigest.co.uk

This book was designed, edited and produced by The
Reader's Digest Association Limited based on material
from *England's Thousand Best Houses* by Simon Jenkins,
first published by Allen Lane, the Penguin Press, a
publishing division of Penguin Books Ltd.

Concept code UK0149/L/S
Book code 634-001-01
ISBN 0 276 44066 8
Oracle code 356600001H.00.24